New
VEGETARIAN
food

New
VEGETARIAN
food

Christine McFadden

PHOTOGRAPHS BY MARIE-LOUISE AVERY

PUBLISHED BY
SALAMANDER BOOKS LIMITED
LONDON

Published by Salamander Books Ltd.
8 Blenheim Court
Brewery Road
London N7 9NY

© Salamander Books Ltd., 2001

A member of the Chrysalis Group plc

ISBN 0 86101 963 6

5 7 9 8 6

Managing Editor: ANNE MCDOWALL
Copy Editor: VERONICA SPERLING
Designer: PETER BRIDGEWATER
Photographer: MARIE-LOUISE AVERY
Home Economist: MEG JANSZ
Stylist: GLORIA NICOL
Typesetting: CHRIS LANAWAY
Illustrator: LORRAINE HARRISON
Indexer: ALISON LEACH
Colour reproduction:
P & W GRAPHICS PTE LTD, SINGAPORE
Printed in Slovenia

CONTENTS

AUTHOR'S ACKNOWLEDGMENT

*I would like to thank my husband, Ed, for his tireless washing up during
the recipe testing. Many thanks also to Veronica Sperling, who edited this
book, and to Alix Pirani, Anna Parry-Jones, Alex Roberts and Ulf and
Wendy Martensson for their love and support throughout the project.*

INTRODUCTION

Vegetarian cooking today is a very different affair from the brown rice and nut roasts of the 70s and early 80s. It is exciting and colourful, and focuses on taste and quality. In this book, my aim is to capture the vitality of new vegetarian cooking, and I hope it will inspire vegetarians and non-vegetarians alike to experiment and to share my passion for the wealth of vegetables, grains, herbs, spices and oils that are now available.

I have drawn on a diverse range of cuisines, from Eastern Europe to South America, but with an emphasis on Mediterranean-style cooking. The recipes combine the exotic with the traditional but always make use of honest, fresh ingredients that naturally belong together and are not masked by too many interfering flavours.

The first chapter, *Vegetables*, provides perhaps the greatest source of inspiration. With their dazzling variety of colour, texture, flavour and their tremendous versatility, vegetables are too good to be treated as a side dish. Here they are given the credit they deserve.

Grains, Pulses and Nuts explores ingredients as old as civilization itself. Some may be unfamiliar to you but all are delicious and prepared with maximum emphasis on lightness and flavour.

Pasta, Pastry, Pancakes and Breads concentrates on time-honoured staples – flour and water – which create a universal background to so many dishes.

The recipes in the appendix are mainly sauces, relishes and dressings – the elements that accent flavours and bring a dish to life with colour and moistness. Although I have specified the sauce or dressing for each dish where appropriate, there are no hard and fast rules, so don't be afraid to mix and match.

Unfamiliar Ingredients

Some of the ingredients may be unfamiliar and are not to be found in every high street supermarket. In most cases a substitute can be used, but it is worth trying to find the more obscure ingredients so you can experience new flavours and expand your repertoire. One of my greatest pleasures is coming across unfamiliar ingredients in street markets, foreign supermarkets, ethnic shops and good healthfood stores. And there is now an increasing number of specialist mail order food companies which supply unusual flours, grains, dried goods, spices and oils.

Herbs

I have used fresh herbs but you can substitute 1 teaspoon of dried for 1 tablespoon of chopped fresh herbs. Most dried herbs benefit from dry-roasting to intensify the flavour. Place them in a small frying pan without any oil. Heat gently, stirring, until they begin to give off their aroma.

Most supermarkets now sell a reasonable variety of fresh herbs, but there are many neglected varieties with magical flavours, such as lovage, hyssop and savory. These are worth growing yourself – even in a pot on a window-sill. I use a lot of coriander, flat-leafed Italian parsley, rocket and sorrel, which are expensive to buy but easy to grow. Failing that, buy these herbs from ethnic shops where they are normally sold in large bunches.

Spices

As with dried herbs, spices benefit from dry-roasting to intensify their flavour. They lose their potency after a few months so buy them in small quantities and store in airtight containers in a cool, dark cupboard.

Pepper should always be freshly ground unless otherwise stated. For preference I use sea salt flakes. They have a different taste from ordinary sea salt and provide beautiful little bursts of flavour on the tongue.

Lemons and Limes

Lemons and limes add an unmistakable but subtle sharpness to savoury dishes. In most cases they can be interchanged, but limes do have a very special flavour. I have specified zest rather than peel, meaning the thin aromatic outer layer of the fruit rather than the rind. Use a special zesting tool or the fine grid on a grater.

Oils

It's worth investing in good quality extra virgin olive oil, particularly for salads. Groundnut oil is best for frying as it has a high smoke-point. Sunflower, grapeseed and safflower oils are good all-purpose oils that are not too heavy.

Go easy on toasted or dark sesame oil – it's more of a flavouring agent than a cooking oil. Flavour your salads with walnut, almond or hazelnut oil, especially if the salad contains nuts; or experiment with pistachio, pumpkin seed or pine kernel oils – they add a beautiful depth of flavour to a dressing.

Sea Vegetables

Seaweeds, or sea vegetables as they are now called, are sometimes treated with suspicion but these are one of the richest sources of minerals and vitamins needed by the body. Sea vegetables are mostly imported from Japan and are available dried in good health food stores. Used in moderation they add a delicious flavour and texture to food. I have used the milder, sweet-flavoured varieties such as arame, hiziki and nori.

Soy Sauce

I prefer to use the traditionally made Japanese soy sauces such as shoyu or tamari (wheat-free) as they have a comforting, warm, mellow flavour definitely not present in other brands. You can buy shoyu and tamari in good health food stores.

Pulses

Dried beans and chick-peas need soaking for 2-8 hours before cooking. The exact time depends on the age of the pulse as does the cooking time. I have usually specified the dry weight of pulses, but if you use pre-cooked or canned ones, double the quantity.

Some dried beans contain a toxin which can cause severe stomach upsets and even death if not destroyed by cooking. Always boil them rapidly for 15 minutes, then discard the cooking water, rinse and cook.

Nuts

Although I have given quantities for the shelled weight, nuts should ideally be freshly cracked before use. Failing that, buy them in small quantities as they easily become rancid. Store in airtight containers in a cool place. The flavour of nuts becomes much richer if you dry-roast them first. Place a single layer in a roasting tin for 7-10 minutes at 180°C/350°F/gas mark 4, stirring occasionally, until they become golden and give off a warm toasted aroma.

Other Notes

All spoon measures are level
Use fresh herbs in preference to dried
1 tablespoon chopped fresh herbs = 1 teaspoon dried
Always use fresh Parmesan cheese
All eggs are medium unless otherwise stated

VEGETABLES

With their wealth of shapes, sizes and flamboyant colours, I find

vegetables one of the most irresistible ingredients available. Because we

eat different parts of the plant – buds, leaves, stems, flowers, roots

and tubers – vegetables provide an almost limitless variety of tastes,

textures and flavours.

Although the supermarkets provide us with an amazing variety of vegetables

all the year round, I am a great believer in seasonal produce. There is nothing to

beat an early winter parsnip, sweetened by the first frosts, or spring cabbages with crisp, squeaky

leaves, or the first tender broad beans.

Vegetables are one of the major sources of the essential health-promoting vitamins A, C and E, but from the

moment of harvest they begin to lose these valuable nutrients. Although there is nothing

to beat the sheer delight of freshly picked vegetables, you can still retain flavour and

nutrients if you buy your vegetables as you need them. Store them for the shortest

possible time in the salad drawer of the refrigerator or in a cool airy larder.

Do any chopping or slicing just before cooking and avoid soaking

them. Heat also destroys nutrients so I cook most vegetables as

briefly as possible to retain maximum flavour and goodness.

CONTENTS

AUBERGINE AND MUSHROOM SATAY

SERVES 6

RICH AND FILLING, THIS DISH CAN BE SERVED ON ITS OWN
AS A STARTER, OR WITH RICE AS A MAIN COURSE.

18 chestnut mushrooms, wiped	*Oil for brushing*
1 large aubergine (about	
350g/12oz)	

MARINADE

6 tbsp olive oil	*1 garlic clove, crushed*
3 tbsp soy sauce	*salt and pepper*
1 tbsp wine vinegar	

TO SERVE

shredded chinese leaves	*Satay Sauce (page 108)*
cucumber, cut into matchstick	
strips	

GARNISH

2 tbsp finely chopped coriander

❖ Cut the mushrooms in half. Cut the aubergine into 2 cm/¾ inch slices then cut each slice into 4 segments. Place the vegetables in a single layer in a non-metallic dish.

❖ Mix together the marinade ingredients and spoon over the vegetables, making sure they are thoroughly coated. Leave for at least 1 hour, turning occasionally.

❖ Thread alternate pieces of mushroom and aubergine on to 12 skewers. Brush with oil and place under a preheated hot grill or on a barbecue. Grill for 10 minutes, turning frequently and brushing with oil, until nicely browned.

❖ Place on a bed of Chinese leaves and cucumber strips. Spoon over some of the satay sauce and serve the rest in a bowl. Sprinkle with coriander and serve immediately.

KOHLRABI CARPACCIO

SERVES 4

POPULAR IN CENTRAL AND EASTERN EUROPE, KOHLRABI IS A
MEMBER OF THE CABBAGE FAMILY BUT LOOKS LIKE A
TURNIP. IT CAN BE EATEN RAW OR COOKED. BUY IT WHEN
IT IS NO BIGGER THAN AN APPLE – LARGER SPECIMENS
TEND TO BE VERY HARD.

3 small kohlrabi, peeled	*salt and pepper*
(weighing about 75 g/3 oz each)	*3 tbsp extra virgin olive oil*
4 large radishes	*1 tbsp walnut oil*
1 large carrot	*1 tbsp snipped chives*
2 tsp orange juice	*25 g/1 oz shelled walnuts,*
2 tsp lime juice	*chopped coarsely*

❖ Using a mandoline or very sharp knife, slice the kohlrabi, radishes and carrot horizontally into paper-thin circles. Place in a shallow serving bowl.

❖ Whisk the citrus juices with the salt, pepper and oils. Pour the dressing over the vegetables and toss well. Leave to stand for 1 hour at room temperature.

❖ Add the chives and walnuts just before serving.

AUBERGINE STIR-FRY WITH HOT SOUR SAUCE

SERVES 4

THE AUBERGINES BECOME SOFT AND SWEET WHEN STIR-
FRIED – A PLEASING CONTRAST TO THE CRISP WATER
CHESTNUTS AND THE SHARP SAUCE.

2 aubergines, peeled
2 red peppers, cored, seeded and
cut into matchstick strips
6 tbsp groundnut oil
100 g/4 oz water chestnuts,
sliced
6 spring onions, sliced
diagonally into 2 cm/¾ inch
lengths
2.5 cm/1 inch piece fresh root
ginger, chopped very finely
2 garlic cloves, chopped
very finely

1 fresh green chilli, deseeded
and chopped very finely
2 tsp sugar
1½ tbsp soy sauce
150 ml/¼ pint Vegetable
Stock (page 111)
2 tsp cornflour, blended with
a little water or stock
1½ tbsp rice vinegar (or white
wine vinegar)
1 tsp sesame seeds

GARNISH
chopped spring onion tops

❖ Slice the aubergines in half lengthways. With the flat side facing downwards, slice each half lengthways into 5 mm/¼ inch strips. Slice the wider strips lengthways in half again, then cut all the strips crossways into 4 cm/1½ inch pieces.

❖ Heat 5 tablespoons of the oil in a wok or large frying pan until almost smoking. Add the aubergine and pepper strips and stir-fry over a high heat for 2-3 minutes until just beginning to colour. Remove from the pan and drain on paper towels.

❖ Heat the remaining oil and stir-fry the water chestnuts, spring onion, ginger, garlic and chilli over a high heat for 1 minute.

❖ Return the aubergine and pepper to the pan and add the sugar, soy sauce and stock. Stir-fry for 2 minutes over a medium heat.

❖ Add the cornflour and cook for a minute, stirring, until thickened slightly. Stir in the vinegar and sesame seeds and stir-fry for 30 seconds more.

❖ Garnish with spring onion tops and serve with boiled rice.

AVOCADO AND CHILLI DIP

SERVES 4

USE A GOOD VARIETY OF HERBS – ANY OR ALL OF THE
FOLLOWING WOULD BE FINE: LOVAGE, ROCKET, SORREL,
SAVORY, THYME, PARSLEY, BASIL, CHIVES AND TARRAGON.

1 fat green fresh chilli
2 medium-sized ripe avocados
1 tbsp lime juice
grated zest of 1 lime
3 tbsp finely chopped mixed
herbs

75 g/3 oz ricotta cheese
1 garlic clove, crushed
2 tsp green peppercorns,
crushed
¼ tsp coarse sea salt
herb sprigs, to garnish

❖ Place the chilli under a hot grill for 5-8 minutes, turning frequently, until the skin blisters and blackens. Remove the skin and seeds and chop the flesh roughly.

❖ Peel the avocados and chop the flesh roughly. Mix with the lime juice to prevent discoloration.

❖ Put the avocado in a food processor with the chilli and remaining ingredients and blend until smooth.

❖ Season to taste, adding more lime juice if necessary, and pour into a serving bowl. Garnish with sprigs of herbs.

❖ If not serving immediately, sprinkle with lime juice, cover tightly and chill. Serve with pumpernickel or rye bread triangles.

GREEN BEAN AND ROASTED GARLIC SALAD

SERVES 6

IT IS WELL WORTH ROASTING THE GARLIC FOR THE WONDERFULLY MELLOW FLAVOUR. ROAST MORE CLOVES THAN YOU NEED AND USE THEM TO FLAVOUR OLIVE OILS AND VINEGARS.

225 g/8 oz fine green beans
175 g/6 oz cherry tomatoes, halved
1 tbsp finely chopped basil
4 tbsp extra virgin olive oil
1 tbsp balsamic vinegar
1 tbsp lime juice
salt and pepper
1 tbsp pine kernels
3 large garlic cloves, unpeeled and left whole
1 head of escarole

❖ Steam the beans over boiling water for 4 minutes until just tender but still crunchy. Refresh under cold water, drain and pat dry with paper towel. Slice in half and place in a bowl with the tomatoes and basil.
❖ Whisk the olive oil with the vinegar, lime juice, salt and pepper. Pour over the bean mixture.
❖ Put the pine kernels on a baking sheet and toast in the oven at 180°C/350°F/gas mark 4 for 2 minutes until golden brown.
❖ Increase the heat to 220°C/425°F/gas mark 7 and roast the garlic for 15 minutes. Remove the skins, chop roughly and add to the beans and tomatoes.
❖ Arrange the escarole leaves on a serving dish and pile the bean mixture on top. Scatter with pine kernels and serve.

BAKED PEPPERS WITH FETA

SERVES 4

SERVE THIS DISH WITH A CRISP GREEN SALAD AS A LIGHT LUNCH OR SUPPER.

1 each large red, green and yellow pepper
salt and pepper
2 garlic cloves, chopped very finely
2 tsp each finely chopped marjoram and parsley
1 tsp finely chopped rosemary
50 g/2 oz fresh wholemeal breadcrumbs
grated zest of 1 lemon
2-3 tbsp olive oil
6 black olives, stoned and sliced
25 g/1 oz feta cheese, cut into 1 cm/½ inch cubes

❖ Place the peppers under a hot grill for 8-10 minutes, turning occasionally, until the skins begin to blacken. Cover or place in a sealed plastic bag for 5 minutes to loosen the skin. Remove the skin, core and seeds.
❖ Cut the flesh into bite-sized pieces and place in a shallow ovenproof dish. Season with salt and pepper.
❖ Combine the garlic, herbs, breadcrumbs and lemon zest. Season with pepper and add the olive oil to bind the mixture together.
❖ Scatter the mixture over the peppers. Add the olives and feta cheese.
❖ Bake in the oven at 220°C/425°F/gas mark 7 for 10-15 minutes until crisp.

CARROT AND LOVAGE SOUP

SERVES 6

LOVAGE IS ONE OF THOSE OLD-FASHIONED HERBS WHICH COULD BE USED MORE OFTEN. IT HAS AN ASTRINGENT FLAVOUR, SLIGHTLY REMINISCENT OF LIQUORICE. IF YOU CAN'T GET HOLD OF IT, USE BASIL OR CELERY LEAVES, OR A MIXTURE OF BOTH.

50 g/2 oz butter
1 onion, chopped
450 g/1 lb carrots, sliced
225 g/8 oz potatoes, sliced

4 tbsp finely chopped lovage
1.2 litres/2 pints Vegetable
Stock (page 111)
salt and pepper

GARNISH
6 tbsp mild yogurt | *lovage leaves*

❖ Melt the butter in a large pan. Add the onion, carrot, potato and lovage. Cover and sweat over a low heat for 10 minutes, stirring occasionally.
❖ Add the stock and season with salt and pepper. Bring to the boil, then simmer for 15 minutes.
❖ Liquidize the mixture until smooth. Reheat gently and check the seasoning.
❖ Serve each bowl with a swirl of yogurt and garnish with a lovage leaf.

MINTED MANGETOUT MOUSSE

SERVES 6

A DELICATELY FLAVOURED FIRST COURSE FOR A SUMMER DINNER. SERVE IT WITH TRIANGLES OF RYE BREAD OR MELBA TOAST, AND CHILLED WHITE WINE.

275 g/10 oz mangeout, trimmed
400 ml/14 fl oz cold Vegetable
Stock (page 110)
¼ tsp sugar
¼ tsp salt
pepper
3 tbsp mayonnaise

250 g/9 oz ricotta cheese
125 ml/4 fl oz double cream
4 heaped tsp Gelozone
(vegetarian gelatine)
4 tbsp finely chopped mint
2 tbsp lemon juice

GARNISH
6 mint sprigs

❖ Put the mangetout in a saucepan. Bring 100 ml/3½ fl oz of the stock to the boil in another pan and pour over the mangetout. Cover and simmer rapidly for 2 minutes, taking care that the liquid does not evaporate. The mangetout should still be crisp and bright green.
❖ Liquidize the mangetout with the cooking liquid, sugar, salt and pepper until smooth.
❖ Beat together the mayonnaise, ricotta and cream.
❖ Put the remaining cold stock in a saucepan. Sprinkle over the Gelozone and stir until completely dissolved. Heat gently, stirring, until the mixture begins to steam. Do not allow to boil.
❖ Beat the dissolved Gelozone into the ricotta mixture, then fold in the mangetout purée, mint and lemon juice. Add more salt and pepper if necessary.
❖ Pour into six 150 ml/¼ pint ramekins, cover and chill. Garnish with a mint sprig before serving.

❖🥕❖✒❖

CELERIAC AND DILL SOUP

SERVES 4-6

CELERIAC IS A SADLY NEGLECTED VEGETABLE
WHICH DESERVES TO BE USED MORE WIDELY. WITH ITS
FRESH, NUTTY FLAVOUR, IT MAKES A WELCOME ADDITION
TO WINTER SALADS.

50 g/2 oz butter or margarine	900 ml/1½ pints Strong
1 bay leaf	Vegetable Stock (page 111)
2 tbsp chopped dill	salt and pepper
1 onion, chopped finely	3 tbsp single cream
1 medium celeriac (about 550 g/	2 tsp lemon juice
1¼ lb), cut into small cubes	

❖ Melt the butter in a saucepan with the bay leaf and half the dill. Simmer over a gentle heat for a minute or two to allow the flavours to develop.

❖ Add the onion and celeriac, cover and simmer gently for about 10 minutes until they begin to soften.

❖ Add the stock and seasoning. Bring to the boil, cover and simmer for about 30 minutes until the vegetables are tender. Remove the bay leaf.

❖ Liquidize the mixture then return to the pan and reheat. Remove from the heat, stir in the cream, lemon juice and remaining dill. Check the seasoning and serve.

GOLDEN GAZPACHO SOUP

SERVES 6

PREPARE THIS SUNSHINE-COLOURED SOUP ONE DAY AHEAD.
YOU CAN USE RED TOMATOES BUT THE COLOUR OF THE
SOUP WILL BE DIFFERENT.

2 x 1.5 cm/½ inch slices white	2 tender celery stalks, leaves
bread, crusts removed, cubed	included, chopped roughly
3 tbsp olive oil	500 g/18 oz yellow cherry
3 tbsp white wine vinegar	tomatoes
few drops of Tabasco sauce	700 ml/1¼ pints cold
3 large yellow peppers	Vegetable Stock (page 111)
1 small onion, unpeeled	½ tsp sugar
2 large garlic cloves, unpeeled	½ tbsp lemon juice
½ cucumber, peeled, seeded and	salt and pepper
chopped roughly	

TO SERVE

1 red pepper, cored, deseeded	9 spring onions, chopped finely
and diced finely	basil sprigs, to garnish
½ cucumber, peeled and	
diced finely	

❖ Put the bread cubes on a baking sheet and bake at 180°C/350°F/gas mark 4 for about 10 minutes until pale golden. Allow to cool then transfer to a large bowl. Increase the temperature to 200°C/400°F/gas mark 6.

❖ Whisk together the oil, vinegar and Tabasco sauce. Pour over the bread, turning the cubes to coat. Leave to stand for 1 hour, turning occasionally.

❖ Place the peppers and onion on a baking sheet and roast for 20 minutes, turning occasionally. Add the garlic and roast for 15 minutes until all the vegetables are tender.

❖ Allow to cool, then skin and deseed the peppers and peel the onion and garlic. Transfer to a food processor with the bread cubes and process to a chunky purée. Pour into a large bowl.

❖ Purée the cucumber, celery and tomatoes for 3 minutes. Push through a sieve, extracting as much moisture as possible. Add the strained vegetables to the bread mixture, mixing well. The mixture should be quite thick. Season to taste with salt and pepper. Cover and chill overnight.

❖ Just before serving, add the sugar and lemon juice and check the seasoning. Ladle into bowls, garnish with a sprig of basil and serve with the diced vegetables.

STEAMED ROOTS WITH CHARGRILLED TOMATO AND CHILLI SAUCE

SERVES 4

A SATISFYING AND FILLING WINTER DISH. BE ADVENTUROUS WITH YOUR SELECTION OF ROOT VEGETABLES AND INCLUDE SOME OF THE LESSER KNOWN VARIETIES – OR YOU CAN USE ONE SORT ONLY. YOU'LL NEED A TOTAL OF ABOUT 1.4 KG/3 LB.

½ celeriac	1 eddo or colocassi (a Greek
2 potatoes	Cypriot root vegetable)
1 parsnip	40 g/1½ oz butter
2 kohlrabi	2 tbsp finely chopped flat-
½ sweet potato	leafed parsley
	salt and pepper

SAUCE

900 g/2 lb plum tomatoes	½ onion, chopped very finely
4 large garlic cloves, unpeeled	½ tsp sugar
2 fresh green chillies	½ tsp salt
2 tsp dried oregano or thyme	pepper
2 tbsp olive oil	15 g/½ oz butter

❖ To make the sauce, place the tomatoes, garlic and chillies under a hot grill. Turn frequently, until the skins blister and blacken. The chillies will need about 5 minutes, the garlic 10-15 minutes and the tomatoes 15-20 minutes.

❖ Peel the garlic, remove the skin and seeds from the chilli, but do not peel the tomatoes.

❖ Dry-fry the oregano in a small heavy-based pan for a few minutes until you can smell the aroma.

❖ Heat the oil in another small pan. Gently fry the onion for about 5 minutes until translucent. Add the oregano and fry for another minute.

❖ Purée the tomatoes, including any blackened bits of skin (they add to the flavour), with the garlic, chilli and onion mixture until smooth.

❖ Pour into a large frying pan and season with the sugar, salt and pepper. Simmer for 5-10 minutes, stirring occasionally, until some of the liquid has evaporated. Stir in the butter and set aside.

❖ Meanwhile, peel the vegetables and cut into even-sized 5 mm/¼ inch thick slices. Place in a steamer set over a large pan of boiling water, putting the denser vegetables at the bottom. Cover tightly and steam for 15 minutes until just tender.

❖ Transfer the vegetables to a heated serving dish. Dot with the butter and carefully stir in the parsley, salt and pepper.

❖ Re-heat the sauce and serve separately.

BAKED CUCUMBER IN DILL AND MINT CREAM

SERVES 4

START THIS DISH AT LEAST THREE HOURS BEFORE YOU PLAN TO SERVE IT, SO THAT THE CUCUMBERS HAVE TIME TO DRAIN PROPERLY.

2 cucumbers	*pepper*
1 tbsp white wine vinegar	*225 ml/8 fl oz double cream*
½ tsp salt	*2 tbsp each finely chopped*
¼ tsp sugar	*dill and mint*
25 g/1 oz butter	*¼ tsp paprika*
2 spring onions, bulb and top,	
chopped finely	

GARNISH

dill leaves	*paprika*

❖ Peel the cucumbers, cut in 4 lengthways and remove the seeds. Cut lengthways into 5 mm/¼ inch strips, then cut across into 5 cm/2 inch pieces.

❖ Place in a large bowl and toss with vinegar, salt and sugar. Leave to stand for 2 hours. Drain and pat dry on paper towels.

❖ Transfer the cucumber pieces to a shallow ovenproof dish. Melt the butter and pour it over the cucumber. Stir in the spring onions and season with plenty of freshly ground black pepper. Bake at 180°C/350°F/gas mark 4, stirring occasionally, for 45 minutes until just tender.

❖ Meanwhile, bring the cream to the boil in a small saucepan. Stir in the dill, mint and paprika. Reduce the heat and simmer for about 10 minutes until the cream has reduced. Season to taste with salt and pepper.

❖ Pour the cream over the cucumber and garnish with dill leaves and a sprinkling of paprika.

CELERIAC, APPLE AND SORREL SALAD

SERVES 4

CELERIAC HAS A LOVELY FRESH, NUTTY TASTE WHICH GOES WELL WITH THE LEMONY SHARPNESS OF SORREL. TO AVOID BRUISING, TEAR THE SORREL LEAVES RATHER THAN CUTTING WITH A KNIFE. IF SORREL IS UNAVAILABLE, USE YOUNG SPINACH LEAVES OR ROCKET INSTEAD.

2 small celeriac, weighing about	*75 g/3 oz young sorrel, stalks*
700 g/1½ lb total	*removed and torn into shreds*
lemon juice	*40 g/1½ oz shelled walnuts,*
2 crisp red-skinned apples	*chopped*

DRESSING

1 tbsp lemon juice	*pepper*
½ tsp sugar	*3 tbsp extra virgin olive oil*
½ tsp Dijon mustard	*1 tbsp walnut oil*
¼ tsp celery salt	

❖ Peel the celeriac and cut into 1 cm/½ inch slices, sprinkling with lemon juice to prevent discoloration.

❖ Plunge into salted boiling water to which you have added 2 tablespoons of lemon juice. Bring back to the boil for 2 minutes.

❖ Drain under cold running water and pat dry with paper towels.

❖ Cut the slices into 1 cm/½ inch dice and place in a salad bowl.

❖ Quarter and core the unpeeled apples, then cut into small dice, sprinkling with lemon juice as you work.

❖ Mix the apple with the celeriac and add the sorrel and nuts.

❖ Whisk together the dressing ingredients. Pour over the salad just before serving and toss gently.

ROASTED LEEKS AND CARROTS

SERVES 4

*THE LEEKS SHOULD BE BROWN
ON THE OUTSIDE AND TENDER INSIDE.*

*2 long carrots, cut lengthways
into eighths*
*8 small leeks, trimmed and left
whole*
*1 small garlic clove, chopped
finely*

*pinch of dried herbes de
Provence*
50 ml/ 2 fl oz olive oil
coarse sea salt
*1 tbsp finely chopped flat-
leafed parsley*

❖ Pack the leeks and carrots closely together in a shallow ovenproof dish just large enough to hold them in a single layer. Scatter the garlic and herbes de Provence over the top. Add the olive oil, turning the vegetables to make sure they are well-coated. Sprinkle with coarse sea salt.

❖ Place in the top of the oven at 250°C/500°F/gas mark 9 and roast for 10 minutes. Turn and roast for another 10 minutes until beginning to blacken. Scatter with parsley and a little more sea salt to taste and serve immediately.

ONION AND POTATO FRITTATA
WITH SALSA VERDE

SERVES 4 - 6

*A FRITTATA IS AN ITALIAN OPEN OMELETTE,
COOKED UNTIL FIRM. SERVE HOT OR AT ROOM
TEMPERATURE ACCOMPANIED BY A SALAD OF MIXED
LEAVES AND PIQUANT GREEN SAUCE.*

3 tbsp olive oil
75 g/3 oz butter
*2 onions, halved and thinly
sliced*
*275 g/10 oz cooked waxy
potatoes, cut into 1 cm/½ inch
cubes*
*25 g/1 oz shelled walnuts,
chopped roughly*

salt and pepper
8 eggs
*40 g/1½ oz freshly grated
Parmesan*
*2 tbsp finely chopped mixed
herbs e.g. thyme, basil, lovage,
tarragon*

TO SERVE
Salsa Verde (Piquant Green Sauce) (page 106)

❖ Heat 2 tablespoons of the olive oil and half the butter in a 25.5 cm/10 inch non-stick frying pan. Gently fry the onions over a medium-low heat for about 40 minutes until very soft, stirring frequently.

❖ Meanwhile, heat the remaining olive oil and 25 g/1 oz of the butter in a pan. Gently fry the potatoes over a medium heat for about 2 minutes, then add the walnut pieces. Continue to fry until the potatoes are golden on all sides – another 3 minutes or so.

❖ Combine the onions, potatoes and walnuts in a bowl. Season with salt and pepper and allow to cool a little.

❖ Beat the eggs well then stir in the Parmesan cheese, ¼ tsp salt, pepper, herbs and the onion mixture.

❖ Wipe out the pan in which you cooked the onions. Heat the remaining butter until foaming. Quickly pour in the egg mixture, stirring with a fork to spread out the filling.

❖ Cover and cook over a low heat for 5-8 minutes until the eggs are almost set. Place briefly under a hot grill until the surface is set but not brown. Slide on to a plate, cut into wedges and serve with the sauce.

SAUTEED MUSHROOMS AND JERUSALEM ARTICHOKES WITH SAGE

SERVES 4

USE A SELECTION OF WILD MUSHROOMS OR CULTIVATED CHESTNUT, LARGE FLAT CAP, SHIITAKE AND OYSTER MUSHROOMS. BE CAREFUL NOT TO OVERCOOK THE ARTICHOKES AS THEY TEND TO DISINTEGRATE.

350 g/12 oz Jerusalem artichokes
50 g/2 oz butter
4 tbsp olive oil
4 tbsp finely chopped fresh sage
550 g/1¼ lb mushrooms, cleaned and cut into bite-sized pieces

2 garlic cloves, chopped finely
salt and pepper
2 tbsp lemon juice
1 tbsp finely chopped parsley
triangles of fried bread and salad of mixed bitter leaves, to serve

❖ Peel the artichokes and cut into 1 cm/½ inch chunks, placing in acidulated water to prevent browning.
❖ Heat half the butter and half the oil in a large frying pan. Add half the sage and fry for 30 seconds to flavour the oil. Add the artichokes and gently fry for 5-6 minutes until just beginning to colour. Season and remove from the pan.
❖ Heat the remaining butter and olive oil and fry the remaining sage for 30 seconds. Add the mushrooms and stir-fry over a high heat for 7-10 minutes, or until most of the liquid has evaporated.
❖ Add the garlic, lemon juice and artichokes. Season generously with salt and pepper and stir-fry for another 1-2 minutes. Sprinkle with the parsley and serve with fried bread triangles and salad.

VEGETABLES ROASTED WITH VINEGAR AND ROSEMARY

SERVES 4-6

THIS SERVES 4 ON ITS OWN OR 6 AS AN ACCOMPANYING DISH. IT IS DELICIOUS WITH ANY TYPE OF CASSEROLE.

8 small potatoes
4 small onions
2 small parsnips, cut into 5 cm/2 inch lengths
2 large carrots, cut into 5 cm/2 inch lengths
4 Jerusalem artichokes
1 small butternut squash, peeled, deseeded and cut into 4 cm/1½ inch cubes
50 g/2 oz unsalted butter, melted
2 tbsp olive oil

3 tbsp balsamic vinegar
2-3 sprigs rosemary
sugar
1 tsp coriander seeds, crushed
coarse sea salt and coarsely ground black pepper
2 tbsp dry vermouth
200 ml/7 fl oz Strong Vegetable Stock (page 111)
1 tsp cornflour, blended with a little water or stock
flat-leafed parsley, to garnish

❖ Steam the vegetables together over boiling water for 5-7 minutes until just beginning to become tender. Place in a roasting pan large enough to hold them in a single layer.
❖ Gently heat together the butter, olive oil, vinegar and rosemary and pour over the vegetables. Sprinkle with a pinch of sugar and the coriander seeds and season generously with the salt and pepper, turning the vegetables until well coated.
❖ Roast in the oven at 180°C/350°F/gas mark 4, for about 1 hour, until evenly browned, basting and turning frequently. Transfer the vegetables to a heated serving dish.
❖ Place the roasting pan over a medium heat and pour in the vermouth and stock. Bring to the boil, scraping up any sediment from the bottom of the pan. Simmer for a few minutes, then season with salt, pepper and a pinch more sugar. Add the cornflour and stir continuously until thickened. Strain and pour the gravy over the vegetables.

BROCCOLI AND WATER CHESTNUT SALAD

SERVES 4

MARINATING THIS DISH WILL ALLOW THE FLAVOURS TO DEVELOP. HOWEVER, IF YOU'RE IN A HURRY IT'S JUST AS DELICIOUS WHILE STILL WARM.

300 g/11 oz broccoli florets
100 g/4 oz water chestnuts, halved
1 tbsp rice vinegar (or white wine vinegar)

2 tbsp tamari (Japanese soy sauce)
3 tbsp extra virgin olive oil
1 cm/½ inch piece fresh root ginger, crushed in a garlic press
½ tbsp sesame seeds, toasted

❖ Steam the broccoli florets over boiling water for 3-5 minutes until bright green and still crisp. Put in a bowl with the water chestnuts.

❖ Whisk together the remaining ingredients, season and pour over the broccoli, turning well to coat.

❖ Cover and leave to marinate at room temperature for at least 1 hour before serving.

ROCKET AND GRILLED PEPPER SALAD WITH PARMESAN CHEESE

SERVES 4

THE PEPPERY FLAVOUR OF THE ROCKET BALANCES THE SWEETNESS OF THE PEPPER.

1 red pepper
50 g/2 oz trimmed rocket
1 garlic clove, diced finely
2 tsp balsamic vinegar

salt and pepper
5 tbsp extra virgin olive oil
40 g/1½ oz fresh Parmesan in one piece

❖ Place the pepper under a hot grill for about 15 minutes, turning occasionally, until blackened on all sides. Remove the skin, core and seeds, then slice into matchstick strips.

❖ Combine the garlic, vinegar, salt and pepper then whisk in the olive oil. Using a swivel peeler, shave the Parmesan cheese into wafers.

❖ Place the rocket on 4 plates and arrange the pepper strips on top. Pour a little dressing over the leaves. Sprinkle with Parmesan shavings and serve at once.

RAGOUT OF YOUNG VEGETABLES

SERVES 6

SERVE WITH CRUSTY BREAD AS A
STARTER, OR AS A MAIN COURSE WITH FRESH PASTA.

100 g/4 oz butter	*175 g/6 oz sugar snap peas, or*
6 baby onions, halved	*mangetout*
lengthways	*450 g/1 lb young broad beans,*
2-3 sprigs of thyme	*shelled and outer skin removed*
4 dwarf patty pan squash,	*2 tbsp finely chopped*
halved, or 8 baby courgettes	*mixed herbs*
15 baby carrots	*juice of 1 lemon*
8 baby sweetcorn ears	*1 garlic clove, chopped finely*
225 g/8 oz thin asparagus, cut	*salt and pepper*
into 5 cm/2 inch lengths	

❖ Bring a large saucepan of salted water to the boil.

❖ Melt 25 g/1 oz of the butter in a large sauté pan. Add the onions, thyme, 175 ml/6 fl oz water and a pinch of salt. Bring to the boil, cover and simmer for 5 minutes.

❖ Meanwhile, blanch the vegetables separately in the order listed, allowing 2 minutes each for the squash and carrots and 1 minute each for the other vegetables. Make sure the water comes back to the boil before adding each one.

❖ As each batch of vegetables is blanched, remove with a slotted spoon and add to the onions. Stir, cover and continue to simmer. Add a little more water if the mixture becomes dry.

❖ When all the vegetables are in the pan, stir in the herbs, lemon juice, garlic and remaining butter. Season to taste. Stir over a high heat until the butter melts and the sauce thickens slightly.

FENNEL AND CARROT SALAD

SERVES 4

A CRUNCHY AND REFRESHING SALAD WHICH IS JUST AS
DELICIOUS MADE WITH CHICORY INSTEAD OF FENNEL.

2 fennel bulbs	*2 tbsp orange juice, strained*
3 carrots	*6 tbsp extra virgin olive oil*
2 tbsp pine kernels, toasted	*salt and pepper*
1 tbsp white wine vinegar	*2-3 heads Little Gem lettuce*

GARNISH
snipped fennel leaves

❖ Cut off the base and top of the fennel, reserving the feathery green leaves. Remove the tough outer layers then cut each bulb lengthwise into 4. Cut away the woody centre then slice the segments lengthwise into narrow strips. Place in a bowl.

❖ Peel the carrots and cut in half crosswise. Using a swivel peeler, shave away wide ribbons of carrot, working from opposite sides. Mix the carrot ribbons with the fennel and add the toasted pine kernels.

❖ Whisk together the vinegar, orange juice, oil and seasoning. Pour over the carrot mixture, tossing well to coat.

❖ Arrange the lettuce leaves around the edge of a shallow serving dish. Pile the carrot mixture on top and garnish with snipped fennel leaves.

ROASTED CHILLI ROULADE

SERVES 6

AN IMPRESSIVE MAIN COURSE AND NOT AS DIFFICULT AS IT
LOOKS. JUST BE BRAVE WHEN TURNING IT OUT!
THE DISH IS NOT OVERWHELMINGLY HOT –
ROASTING THE CHILLIES MELLOWS THE FLAVOUR AND
THE EGGS CALM DOWN THE HEAT.

350 ml/12 fl oz milk	*75 g/3 oz butter*
½ tsp cumin seeds, toasted	*5 tbsp flour*
1 tsp coriander seeds, toasted	*½ tsp salt*
6 peppercorns	*5 eggs, separated*
4 fat fresh red chillies	*4 tbsp finely chopped coriander*
4 large garlic cloves, unpeeled	*3 tbsp freshly grated Parmesan*

FILLING

200 g/7 oz ricotta cheese	*1 small avocado*
1-2 tbsp milk	*1 tbsp lime juice*
grated zest 1 lime	*10 cherry tomatoes, cut in 6*
salt and pepper	*1 tbsp finely chopped coriander*

GARNISH
cherry tomato slices

TO SERVE
mixed leaf salad

❖ Grease and line a 30 x 30 cm/12 x 12 inch shallow baking tin with well-oiled baking parchment. Sprinkle with flour, knocking off any excess.

❖ Heat the milk in a small saucepan with the cumin, coriander and peppercorns. Leave to infuse for 30 minutes.

❖ Roast the chillies and garlic in the oven at 220°C/425°F/gas mark 7, for 20 minutes, turning occasionally, until the skin begins to blister and blacken. Remove the skin and seeds from the chillies and the skin from the garlic. Chop the flesh roughly.

❖ Melt the butter in a saucepan, add the flour and cook, stirring constantly for 2 minutes. Whisk in the hot strained milk and cook for 3-4 minutes, stirring constantly. Season with the salt and allow to cool a little.

❖ Put the roasted chillies and garlic in a blender with a little of the white sauce and purée until smooth. Stir the mixture into the sauce in the pan.

❖ Beat the egg yolks in a large mixing bowl. Beat in a little of the sauce then gradually beat in the rest. Fold in the chopped coriander and Parmesan cheese.

❖ Stiffly beat the egg whites with a pinch of salt. Using a metal spoon, carefully fold in 1 tablespoon of egg white to slacken the chilli mixture, then fold in the remainder.

❖ Pour the mixture into the prepared tin, spreading it into the corners and levelling the surface. Bake in the oven at 200°C/400°F/gas mark 6 for 15 minutes until brown and puffed.

❖ Allow to settle for a few minutes then turn out on to a clean tea towel. Leave for 5 minutes then carefully remove the parchment. Trim the edges neatly with a sharp knife.

❖ Mix the ricotta with just enough milk to give a spreading consistency. Stir in the lime zest and season to taste. Spread over the base leaving a small margin all round.

❖ Peel and finely dice the avocado and mix with the lime juice, tomato and coriander. Scatter the mixture over the ricotta and season with salt and pepper.

❖ Carefully roll up like a Swiss roll and transfer to a serving dish, seam side down. Garnish with tomato and serve with a mixed leaf salad.

VEGETABLE KEBABS WITH CORIANDER SAUCE

SERVES 4

2 corn-on-the-cob, sliced into 2 cm/³/4 inch rounds
8 firm cherry tomatoes
2 red onions, cut into 3-layer 2.5 cm/1 inch pieces
1 red and 1 yellow pepper, deseeded and cut into 2.5cm/1 inch pieces
8 baby pattypan squash, halved, or 2 small courgettes, cut into 1 cm/¹/2 inch chunks

16 small shiitake mushrooms, stems removed
75 g/3 oz butter
3 tbsp olive oil
1 garlic clove, chopped very finely
¹/2 tsp cumin seeds, crushed
1 tsp coriander seeds, crushed
pinch of cayenne pepper
salt and pepper
Coriander Sauce (page 107), to serve

❖ Prepare the vegetables and thread on to 8 skewers.
❖ Melt the butter with the olive oil, garlic, spices and seasonings.
❖ Brush the kebabs with the melted butter mixture. Place under a hot grill or over a barbecue. Grill for 15 minutes, turning and basting frequently, until just tender and beginning to blacken around the edges.
❖ Serve with the coriander sauce.

GRILLED AUBERGINE SALAD

SERVES 4

THE AUBERGINES BROWN VERY QUICKLY UNDER THE GRILL. TAKE CARE NOT TO BURN THEM.

2 small aubergines
1 red onion
150 ml/¹/4 pint olive oil
¹/4 tsp dried red pepper flakes
¹/2 tsp cumin seeds
¹/2 tsp sesame seeds

2 garlic cloves, chopped very finely
¹/4 tsp salt
pepper
2 tbsp lime juice

DRESSING

150 ml/¹/4 pint Greek yogurt
2 tbsp finely chopped coriander
grated zest of ¹/2 lime

1 garlic clove, chopped very finely
salt and pepper

GARNISH

slices of lime | *coriander leaves*

❖ Cut the aubergine into 1 cm/¹/2 inch slices and the onion into 5 mm/¹/4 inch slices. Keep the onion rings in one piece by inserting 2 cocktail sticks from the outer ring to the centre. Put the aubergine and onion in a large bowl.
❖ Combine the olive oil, red pepper flakes, cumin and sesame seeds, garlic, salt and pepper. Pour the mixture over the aubergine and onion slices, turning to coat. Marinate for at least 30 minutes.
❖ Meanwhile, mix together the yogurt, coriander, lime zest, garlic, salt and pepper. Leave to stand.
❖ Place the vegetables on a rack under a hot grill for about 5 minutes each side, until slightly blackened. Allow to cool.
❖ Remove the cocktail sticks from the onion slices and cut each slice in 4. Cut the small aubergine slices in half and the larger ones in 4.
❖ Mix the onion and aubergine in a serving bowl and sprinkle with the lime juice. Carefully fold in the yogurt mixture. Leave to stand at room temperature for about 1 hour to allow the flavours to develop.
❖ Garnish with lime slices and coriander leaves. Serve with warm naan bread.

ORIENTAL-STYLE RATATOUILLE

SERVES 6

THE VEGETABLES ARE LIGHTLY COOKED TO RETAIN THEIR
SHAPE AND COLOUR. THE DISH MAY BE SERVED HOT OR
COLD AS A STARTER, OR SERVED HOT AS A MAIN COURSE
ACCOMPANIED BY A GRAIN DISH AND A GREEN SALAD.

6 tbsp olive oil
1 small onion, chopped finely
2 garlic cloves, chopped finely
450 g/1 lb ripe plum tomatoes,
peeled and chopped
2 tbsp tamari (Japanese soy
sauce)
1½ tablespoons rice wine (or
dry sherry)
1 tsp sugar
salt and pepper
1 fresh green chilli, deseeded
and chopped finely

2 tsp coriander seeds, toasted
and crushed
1 small aubergine, cut into 2
cm/¾ inch chunks
150 g/5 oz shiitake mushrooms,
sliced thickly
2 small courgettes, cut into 1
cm/½ inch diagonal slices
1 yellow and 1 red pepper,
cored, deseeded and sliced
2 tsp sesame seeds, toasted

❖ Heat 2 tablespoons of the oil in a saucepan. Gently fry the onion for 5 minutes until soft. Add the garlic and fry for 30 seconds. Stir in the tomatoes, tamari, sherry and sugar. Season with salt and pepper to taste.
❖ Simmer over a low heat, stirring occasionally, while you cook the vegetables. The sauce should reduce and thicken slightly.
❖ Heat the remaining oil in a large pan and stir-fry the chilli and coriander seeds for a minute or two.
❖ Add the aubergines and mushrooms and stir-fry over a medium heat for 5 minutes.
❖ Add the remaining vegetables, with more oil if necessary, and stir-fry for 5 minutes.
❖ Stir in the tomato sauce. Cover and simmer for 10 minutes. Season to taste and stir in the sesame seeds.

ROCKET AND PARSLEY SOUP

SERVES 6

USE FLAT-LEAFED PARSLEY AS IT HAS A BETTER FLAVOUR.
IF YOU CAN'T GET HOLD OF ROCKET, MAKE THE SOUP WITH
PARSLEY INSTEAD.

175 g/6 oz flat-leafed parsley
50 g/2 oz butter
250 g/9 oz potatoes, sliced
250 g/9 oz leeks, sliced
250 g/9 oz celery, sliced

1.3 litres/2¼ pints Vegetable
Stock (page 111)
175 g/6 oz rocket
200 ml/7 fl oz single cream
salt and pepper

TO SERVE
fried bread croûtons

❖ Remove the stalks from the parsley and chop them.
❖ Melt the butter in a large saucepan. Add the chopped parsley stalks, potatoes, leeks and celery. Cover and sweat over a low heat for about 10 minutes, stirring occasionally.
❖ Add the stock, bring to the boil and simmer for 15 minutes.
❖ Roughly chop a handful of parsley and rocket leaves and set aside. Add the remaining leaves to the pan, bring to the boil and simmer for a minute or two. The leaves should remain bright green.
❖ Liquidise the mixture then pass through a sieve and return to the pan. Season to taste. Add the cream and reheat gently. Check the seasoning.
❖ Garnish each bowl with the reserved chopped leaves and serve with croûtons.

PRESSED SPINACH AND GOAT CHEESE TERRINE WITH NORI

SERVES 8

A COLOURFUL AND REFRESHING DISH FOR A SUMMER DINNER. START IT THE DAY BEFORE YOU PLAN TO SERVE IT AND BE PREPARED TO SPEND AN HOUR OR SO ON THE PREPARATION. NORI IS A DELICATELY FLAVOURED JAPANESE SEA VEGETABLE NORMALLY USED FOR MAKING SUSHI ROLLS. SOME BRANDS ARE ALREADY PRE-TOASTED, OTHERWISE WAVE THE SHEETS OVER A GAS FLAME OR PLACE UNDER A HOT GRILL FOR A FEW SECONDS.

16-18 spinach leaves, stems removed, or 150 g/5 oz trimmed bakchoy leaves
2 large yellow peppers
1 fennel bulb, trimmed, quartered and separated into layers
12 plum tomatoes with a good flavour

2 x 20.5 cm/8 inch squares toasted nori
pepper
2 tbsp each finely chopped parsley and chives
6-8 torn basil leaves
225 g/8 oz dry goat cheese, crumbled

TO SERVE
mixed leaves e.g. endive, butterhead, lamb's lettuce, radicchio
extra virgin olive oil

❖ Plunge the spinach leaves into boiling water for 30 seconds. Drain and cool completely under cold water. Spread out on paper towels to dry.

❖ Place the peppers under a hot grill for 10 minutes, turning occasionally, until the skins begin to blacken and blister. Place in a sealed plastic bag for 5 minutes then remove the skin, core and seeds. Cut the flesh into match-stick strips.

❖ Plunge the fennel pieces into boiling water for 4 minutes. Drain under cold running water, then dry with paper towels and chop finely.

❖ Put the tomatoes in a bowl, pour over boiling water and leave for 1 minute. Drain and remove the skins. Cut into 5 mm/¼ inch slices, discarding the seeds, then chop roughly and drain.

❖ Line a 20.5 cm/8 inch square cake tin with greased foil. Place a sheet of nori in the bottom of the tin. Cover with a layer of spinach leaves, overlapping them neatly so there are no gaps. Season with pepper and a sprinkling of herbs.

❖ Crumble half the goat cheese over the spinach, followed by half the tomatoes. Season with pepper and add more herbs.

❖ Add the peppers and fennel, spreading out the pieces evenly. Season again with pepper and herbs.

❖ Add the remaining tomatoes and goat cheese and season with pepper and herbs. Gently flatten the mixture, pushing it into the corners and sides of the tin. Top with the remaining spinach leaves.

❖ Place the second sheet of nori on top, pressing it down gently with the palm of your hand. Cover with a double thickness of greased foil. Press down with a heavy weight and chill in the refrigerator for at least 8 hours.

❖ Invert the tin over a chopping board and remove the foil. Cut the terrine into 4 squares, using an electric carving knife if possible. Carefully cut each square in half diagonally.

❖ Arrange a few lettuce leaves on 8 plates and sprinkle with olive oil. Place the triangles of terrine on top.

BEETROOT ROASTED WITH CHILLI, GARLIC AND THYME

SERVES 4

A DISH TO CONVERT EVEN THE MOST HARDENED BEETROOT HATER. USE RAW BEETROOT RATHER THAN PRE-COOKED AS IT HAS A MUCH SUBTLER FLAVOUR. THE SLIGHT SWEETNESS IS OFFSET BY THE CHILLI AND GARLIC.

4 tbsp olive oil
450 g/1 lb raw beetroot, peeled and quartered
salt and pepper
1 tbsp finely chopped thyme, or 1½ tsp dried herbes de Provence

1-2 fresh red chillis, deseeded and chopped roughly
4 large garlic cloves, unpeeled
finely chopped thyme, to garnish

❖ Put the oil in a small roasting tin and place in the oven at 200°C/400°F/gas mark 6 for 5 minutes until very hot.

❖ Add the beetroot, turning well to coat. Season generously with salt and pepper and add the thyme.

❖ Roast for 45 minutes, turning occasionally, then add the chilli and garlic. Roast for another 40 minutes until the garlic is very soft and purée-like.

❖ Remove the garlic skin and stir the purée into the oil. Transfer to a warm serving dish and pour the oil from the tin over the beetroot. Garnish with fresh thyme.

❖ Serve with a green salad and boiled polenta, using the polenta to mop up the delicious garlicky oil.

TRI-COLOUR CABBAGE WITH CORIANDER AND SESAME

SERVES 4

IF YOU DON'T HAVE A STEAMER, COOK THE CABBAGES IN A VERY LITTLE WATER, KEEPING THE RED CABBAGE SEPARATE.

250 g/9 oz each of red, white and savoy cabbage
2 tsp sesame seeds
40 g/1½ oz butter

coarse sea salt
pepper
3 tbsp finely chopped coriander leaves

❖ Cut the cabbage in wedges and slice away the core. Cut crossways into fine slices, discarding any thick ribs.

❖ Place the red cabbage in the bottom of a large steamer basket with the savoy and white cabbage on top. Cover and steam over boiling water for 5 minutes. The cabbage should be tender but still crunchy and the colours bright.

❖ Meanwhile, dry-fry the sesame seeds until the aroma is released. Melt the butter in a small saucepan. Add the sesame seeds.

❖ Making sure any liquid from the red cabbage has dripped from the base of the steamer basket, transfer the cabbage to a heated serving dish. Season generously with sea salt and pepper. Pour the melted butter over the cabbage, sprinkle with the coriander, and toss gently to mix the colours.

TOMATO AND BREAD SOUP

SERVES 4-6

A MEAL IN ITSELF, THIS VERY THICK TUSCAN-STYLE TOMATO SOUP NEEDS ONLY A GREEN SALAD TO ACCOMPANY IT. SERVE WITH PLENTY OF EXTRA BREAD TO WIPE OUT THE BOWLS.

7 tbsp olive oil
1 tbsp finely chopped sage
8 tbsp finely chopped basil
2 onions, chopped finely
225 g/8 oz celery, leaves included, diced finely
225 g/8 oz savoy cabbage, sliced thinly
salt and pepper

4 large garlic cloves, sliced very thinly
2½ tbsp tomato purée
1.4 kg/3 lb canned chopped tomatoes
750 ml/1¼ pints Vegetable Stock (page 111)
175 g/6 oz day-old Italian bread, cut into 2.5 cm/1 inch cubes

TO SERVE
coarsely grated Parmesan

❖ Heat 3 tablespoons of the oil in a large, heavy-based saucepan. Add the sage and half the basil and gently fry for 1 minute to flavour the oil.

❖ Add the onions and gently fry for about 7 minutes until soft. Add the celery, cabbage, garlic and salt and pepper. Gently fry for another 5 minutes.

❖ Stir in the tomato purée, tomatoes and stock. Bring to the boil, then cover and simmer gently for 1½-2 hours, topping up with stock or water if necessary.

❖ Place the bread cubes on a baking sheet and toast in the oven at 150°C/300°F/gas mark 2 for 5 minutes.

❖ Place the bread in a large saucepan. Pour the remaining olive oil over the bread and allow it to soak in.

❖ Pour the broth over the bread and leave to stand for 15 minutes. Reheat gently, stir in the remaining basil and check the seasoning.

❖ Make sure each serving includes some of the bread from the bottom of the pan. Serve with grated Parmesan.

CHICORY AND TOMATO GRATIN

SERVES 4

CHOOSE A DISH JUST BIG ENOUGH TO HOLD THE CHICORY WITHOUT LEAVING GAPS IN BETWEEN.

4 large plump heads of chicory, halved lengthways
salt and pepper
olive oil
2 garlic cloves, chopped finely
200 g/7 oz can chopped tomatoes

2 tsp finely chopped marjoram or basil
40 g/1½ oz dry breadcrumbs
40 g/1½ oz freshly grated Parmesan
50 g/2 oz butter

❖ Make 2 or 3 deep cuts in the base of the chicory heads. With the cut side down, place under a hot grill for 3-5 minutes until just beginning to blacken. Turn over, sprinkle with salt and pepper and brush generously with olive oil, working the oil between the leaves. Grill, cut side upwards, for 10-15 minutes until just tender. Transfer the chicory to a shallow ovenproof dish.

❖ Meanwhile, heat 1 tablespoon of olive oil in a small saucepan. Add the garlic and gently fry for 30 seconds, then add the tomatoes and marjoram. Season to taste with salt and pepper. Simmer for 5 minutes, stirring occasionally, then pour the mixture over the chicory.

❖ Combine the breadcrumbs and Parmesan cheese, then sprinkle it over the chicory. Dot with the butter and bake at 190°C/375°F/gas mark 5 for 10 minutes until crisp.

ROCKET AND PINE KERNEL SOUFFLE

SERVES 4

ROCKET IS WORTH GROWING YOURSELF AS IT IS EXPENSIVE
TO BUY AND USUALLY AVAILABLE ONLY IN SMALL PACKETS.

200 g/7 oz trimmed rocket	*4 tbsp freshly grated Parmesan*
25 g/1 oz pine kernels	*salt and pepper*
75 g/3 oz butter	*4 egg yolks*
2 tbsp flour	*5 egg whites*
175 ml/6 fl oz milk	*⅛ tsp cream of tartar*

TO SERVE
cherry tomato salad

❖ Steam the rocket for 5 minutes until just wilted. Purée in a blender until smooth. Reheat with 25 g/1 oz of the butter.

❖ Toast the pine kernels in the oven at 200°C/400°F/gas mark 6, for 2 minutes until golden brown. Chop roughly and set aside.

❖ Place a metal baking sheet in the oven and maintain the temperature.

❖ Melt the remaining butter in a saucepan. Add the flour and stir to a smooth paste. Gradually add the milk, stirring constantly over a medium heat until it comes to the boil.

❖ Remove from the heat and stir in the puréed rocket, the pine kernels and half the grated Parmesan. Season generously with salt and pepper.

❖ Transfer the mixture to a large bowl then whisk in the egg yolks one at a time.

❖ Beat the egg whites with the cream of tartar until stiff. Fold 1 tablespoon of egg white into the rocket mixture to slacken it. Then carefully fold in the remainder, using a metal spoon.

❖ Grease a 1.7 litre/3 pint soufflé dish and sprinkle it with the remaining Parmesan, tipping out the surplus. Pour in the soufflé mixture and scatter any surplus cheese over the top.

❖ Carefully place the dish on the baking sheet in the oven and gently close the oven door. Immediately reduce the temperature to 190°C/375°F/gas mark 5. Bake for 30 minutes and serve immediately.

WATERCRESS CUSTARDS
WITH CARROT AND ORANGE SAUCE

SERVES 6

A VERY PRETTY FIRST
COURSE WITH CITRUSY UNDERTONES.

3 large bunches watercress, stalks removed (about 175 g/6 oz trimmed) and chopped roughly	*2 large eggs (size 2)*
	2 large egg yolks (size 2)
	300 ml/½ pint double cream
200 ml/7 fl oz Vegetable Stock (page 111)	*grated zest of 1 lemon*
	salt and pepper

SAUCE

150 g/5 oz baby carrots, cut into very thin diagonal slices	*50 g/2 oz butter*
	½ tsp finely chopped rosemary
6 tbsp Vegetable Stock (page 111)	*pinch of sugar*
	salt and pepper
2 tbsp orange juice	*1 tbsp double cream*

GARNISH
6 watercress sprigs

❖ Generously butter 6 x 150 ml/¼ pint oval ramekins and place a piece of buttered greaseproof paper in the bottom of each.

❖ Put the watercress in a saucepan. Bring the stock to the boil in another pan. Pour it over the watercress. Cover and cook rapidly for about 1 minute until the watercress just wilts.

❖ Purée the watercress in a food processor with the cooking liquid and allow to cool a little.

❖ Beat the eggs and yolks, then gradually beat in the watercress purée. Stir in the cream, lemon zest and seasoning.

❖ Pour the mixture into the prepared ramekins. Place in a deep roasting tin with enough hot water to come halfway up their sides and bake in the oven at 180°C/350°F/gas mark 4, for 30-35 minutes until set.

❖ To make the sauce, put the carrots, stock and orange juice in a small saucepan with 15 g/½ oz of the butter, the rosemary, sugar, salt and pepper. Bring to the boil, then simmer gently, uncovered, for 3-4 minutes. The carrots should be underdone.

❖ Dice the remaining butter and add to the pan with the cream. Stir over a medium heat until the butter has melted. Raise the heat and simmer rapidly for 2 minutes until the sauce has reduced and thickened slightly. Remove from the heat and set aside.

❖ Remove the ramekins from the oven and leave to rest for a few minutes. Turn out onto 6 warmed plates.

❖ Garnish with a watercress sprig and 1 or 2 slices of carrot from the sauce. Pour a little of the remaining sauce onto each plate and serve at once.

GREEN BEAN AND KOHLRABI SALAD WITH LEMON GRASS AND MINT

SERVES 4

A TRADITIONAL THAI FLAVOURING, LEMON GRASS HAS A SUBTLE, WARM, LEMONY-LIME FLAVOUR. YOU CAN USE GRATED LEMON ZEST INSTEAD BUT IT IS NOT AS GOOD.

225 g/8 oz fine green beans, trimmed and cut into 5 cm/2 inch pieces
1 kohlrabi, about 100 g/4 oz
75 g/3 oz yellow pepper, cut into 5 mm/¼ inch dice
2 large lemon grass stalks
125 ml/4 fl oz Vegetable Stock (page 111)

1 small garlic clove, chopped finely
½ tsp coriander seeds, toasted and crushed
3 tbsp olive oil
salt and pepper
2 tsp finely chopped mint
½ fresh red chilli, deseeded and sliced very finely, to garnish

❖ Place the beans in a steamer over boiling water and steam for 3-4 minutes until just tender but still crunchy. Drain under cold running water and dry with paper towels.

❖ Peel the kohlrabi and slice thinly. Stack a few slices at a time and cut into matchstick strips.

❖ Put the beans, kohlrabi and yellow pepper in a bowl.

❖ Remove and discard the tough, outer leaves of the lemon grass. Cut the centre crossways into very thin slices. Place in a saucepan with the stock and simmer for 10 minutes.

❖ In a blender, purée the lemon grass and stock with the garlic, coriander, olive oil, salt and pepper until smooth.

❖ Pour the dressing over the vegetables. Add the mint and toss gently. Garnish with finely sliced chilli. Leave to stand.

MUSHROOM AND YELLOW PEPPER SALAD

SERVES 4-6

TRIM THE STALKS FROM THE SHIITAKE MUSHROOMS AS THEY CAN BE QUITE TOUGH. USE A VERY LARGE PAN, OR FRY THE MUSHROOMS IN BATCHES IF NECESSARY.

2 yellow peppers
4 tbsp olive oil
6 tbsp walnut oil
1 tbsp balsamic vinegar
4 tbsp chopped lovage or basil
salt and pepper
350 g/12 oz each oyster and shiitake mushrooms, cut into segments if large

2 garlic cloves, chopped finely
50 g/2 oz walnuts, chopped roughly
1 head radicchio
handful each of lamb's lettuce and rocket

❖ Place the yellow peppers under a hot grill for about 15 minutes, turning occasionally, until blackened on all sides. Remove the skin, core and seeds. Cut the flesh into strips about 4 cm/1½ inch long and place in a shallow dish.

❖ Whisk together the olive oil, 2 tablespoons of the walnut oil, all the vinegar, 3 tablespoons of the lovage, and seasoning. Pour over the pepper strips.

❖ Heat 3 tablespoons of the walnut oil in a large frying pan over a high heat until it begins to smoke. Add the mushrooms and stir-fry for 10 minutes. Add the garlic and stir-fry for another minute.

❖ Add to the peppers in the dish, turning well to coat. Leave to stand at room temperature for at least 1 hour.

❖ Heat the remaining walnut oil, add the walnuts and stir-fry for 1 minute. Remove from the pan and set aside.

❖ Place the salad leaves in a bowl and toss with half the mushroom mixture and half the walnuts. Pile the remaining mixture on top and garnish with the remaining lovage and walnuts.

GRAINS, PULSES AND NUTS

Thousands of years ago, grains and pulses changed the nature of civilization.

Being the first foods that could be stored, they enabled our nomadic ancestors to

establish settled communities and to survive for long periods. No wonder then that grains and

pulses have a quality, almost a life force, unequalled by any other food. There is hardly a country in the world that

does not have a grain or pulse-based dish as part of its traditional cuisine – the rich cassoulets of France, Caribbean

rice and peas, Indian dhal, Mexican refried beans.

The ingredients for these recipes are widely available from wholefood stores and good supermarkets. Yet,

surprisingly, many of them are not a regular part of the Western diet. Quinoa with its beautiful pearly seeds,

succulent wild rice, earthy buckwheat, and even the common yellow split pea, are all sadly neglected. They

are the most versatile of ingredients and I have tried to develop appetising ways of introducing

them, always with an emphasis on lightness and flavour. Delicious on their own, but

naturally bland, pulses and grains combine well with more robust ingredients. Fiery chillies,

coriander, lime juice, spices, tomatoes and garlic all complement the subtle

flavours and mild sweetness of pulses and grains, while they in turn

help to mellow the stronger flavours.

Nuts are another basic staple food which enhance

dishes with their unique flavours and crunchy

texture. The new season's 'wet' walnuts and the

first crisp cobnuts of autumn are sheer delight.

CONTENTS

POLENTA AND BASIL GRATIN

SERVES 4-6

MADE FROM CORNMEAL AND INTRODUCED TO EUROPE FROM
THE NEW WORLD BY COLUMBUS, POLENTA FORMED THE
TRADITIONAL STAPLE DIET IN NORTHERN ITALY. IT IS
CHEAP, COLOURFUL AND VERSATILE AND DEEPLY
SATISFYING TO EAT.

1 litre/1¾ pints water
1½ tsp salt
225 g/8 oz cornmeal (polenta)
8 large basil leaves, torn
25 g/1 oz pine kernels, toasted
375 ml/13 fl oz Tomato Sauce
(page 108)

200 g/7 oz Fontina or
Mozzarella, sliced thinly
75 g/3 oz Gorgonzola, crumbled
75 g/3 oz Parmesan, grated
coarsely
pepper

GARNISH
chopped basil

❖ Put the water and salt in a large saucepan. Whisk in the polenta in a stream to prevent lumps forming and bring to the boil, stirring constantly with a wooden spoon.

❖ Lower the heat and stir vigorously for 2-3 minutes, then cover and simmer for 10 minutes. Continue in this way for about 40 minutes or until the mixture pulls away from the sides of the pan.

❖ Stir in the torn basil leaves and pine kernels. Spread out the mixture in a 1 cm/½ inch thick layer in a dampened shallow dish measuring about 30.5 x 23 cm/12 x 9 inches. Leave to cool then cut into 7.5 x 4 cm/3 x 1½ inch strips.

❖ Lightly grease a shallow baking dish and spread about 225 ml/8 fl oz of the tomato sauce over the bottom. Arrange the polenta and slices of Fontina or Mozzarella in an overlapping layer. Sprinkle with the Gorgonzola then spoon the remaining sauce over the top. Sprinkle with the Parmesan and season with pepper. Bake in the oven at 200°C/400°F/gas mark 6 for 25-30 minutes. Garnish with basil and serve with a green salad.

BROCCOLI AND CHILLI RISOTTO

SERVES 4

TRIM THE BROCCOLI FLORETS WHERE THE STEMS
MEET THE STALK. THE HEADS SHOULD BE NO MORE THAN
2.5 CM/1 INCH ACROSS. KEEP THE STOCK SIMMERING ALL
THE TIME YOU ARE COOKING THE RICE.

225 g/8 oz broccoli florets,
blanched
2 tbsp vegetable oil
40 g/1½ oz butter
50 g/2 oz onion, very finely
chopped
1-2 fresh red chillies, deseeded
and chopped very finely

275 g/10 oz arborio or other
Italian risotto rice
1 l/1¾ pint hot Vegetable Stock
(page 111)
3 tbsp freshly grated Parmesan
salt and pepper

❖ Heat the oil and 15 g/½ oz of the butter in a large non-stick frying pan. Add the onion and chilli and gently fry over a medium heat 5-7 minutes until the onion is translucent. Add the rice and stir over a medium-high heat for 1-2 minutes until all the grains are well-coated.

❖ Pour in 300 ml/½ pint of the hot vegetable stock. Cook over a medium-high heat, stirring constantly, until the liquid has evaporated. Add another 150 ml/¼ pint of the stock and stir again until the liquid has evaporated. Cook for about 25-30 minutes, adding more stock and stirring constantly until the rice is tender but firm to bite. It should be creamy and slightly moist but not too runny.

❖ Remove from the heat and stir in the reserved broccoli, Parmesan, salt and pepper, and the remaining butter.

QUINOA SALAD WITH
CUCUMBER AND PISTACHIO NUTS

SERVES 4

A VERY PRETTY AND DELICATE SALAD, EVEN THOUGH MADE
WITH GRAIN. THE LITTLE QUINOA SEEDS DEVELOP A
BEAUTIFUL PEARLY EDGE WHEN COOKED. BULGAR WHEAT
CAN BE SUBSTITUTED BUT THIS MAKES A HEAVIER DISH.

150 g/5 oz quinoa
350 ml/12 fl oz water
1½ tsp salt
½ cucumber
50 g/2 oz shelled pistachio nuts

100 g/4 oz seedless black grapes,
halved
radicchio and Little Gem
lettuce, to serve

DRESSING
1½ tbsp raspberry vinegar
¼ tsp salt
¼ tsp sugar

2 tbsp olive oil
1 tbsp pistachio oil

❖ Rinse the quinoa in several changes of water until the water becomes clear. Put in a saucepan with the water and 1 teaspoon of the salt. Bring to the boil, cover and simmer gently for about 20 minutes until the water is absorbed.

❖ Spread out the quinoa on a clean cloth and fluff with a fork to separate the grains. Leave to dry for 30 minutes.

❖ Peel away a broad band of skin from either side of the cucumber. Cut into 3 mm/⅛ inch slices. Taking a small pile of slices at a time, cut into matchstick strips so that each strip has a small piece of peel at either end. Cut the strips in half crosswise. Put in a sieve, sprinkle with the remaining salt and leave to drain for 30 minutes.

❖ Pour boiling water over the pistachio nuts, leave for 5 minutes then drain and remove the skins.

❖ Put the quinoa in a bowl with the cucumber, pistachio nuts and grapes.

❖ Whisk the dressing ingredients and add to the bowl, tossing gently. Leave at room temperature for at least 1 hour to allow the flavours to develop.

❖ Arrange the leaves on a shallow serving dish and pile the quinoa salad on top.

AUTUMN NUT AND PEAR SALAD

SERVES 4

THIS IS BEST MADE WITH NEW SEASON NUTS – CRUNCHY
'WET' WALNUTS FROM GRENOBLE OR COBNUTS WHEN THE
SHELLS ARE STILL PALE GREEN AND THE NUTMEAT STILL
CRISP AND MOIST.

2 ripe juicy pears
squeeze of lemon juice
6 tender celery stalks, leaves
included
100 ml/3½ fl oz Pear and
Walnut Oil Dressing (page 109)

75 g/3 oz shelled fresh walnuts
or cobnuts, chopped roughly
handful of trimmed watercress
or rocket, to garnish

❖ Core and dice the pears. Place in a salad bowl and sprinkle with the lemon juice to prevent discoloration.

❖ Cut the celery into diagonal 5 mm/¼ inch slices and add to the pears. Stir in the nuts and dressing.

❖ Scatter the watercress or rocket over the salad and serve.

CHICK-PEA AND AUBERGINE CASSEROLE WITH GROUNDNUTS AND SEEDS

SERVES 6

A HEARTY STEW WITH RICH, EARTHY FLAVOURS FROM THE GROUND NUTS AND SEEDS. SERVE WITH WARM CRUSTY BREAD OR BAKED POTATOES.

200 g/7 oz chick-peas, soaked overnight	*400 g/ 14 oz can chopped tomatoes*
1 tsp cumin seeds	*1 red pepper, diced*
2 tsp coriander seeds	*1 aubergine, cut into 1.5 cm/*
2 tbsp sesame seeds	*¾ inch pieces*
2 tsp dried oregano	*225 g/8 oz green beans, chopped*
25 g/1 oz shelled Brazil nuts or almonds, toasted	*600 ml/1 pint Vegetable Stock (page 111)*
3 tbsp olive oil	*salt*
2 onions, chopped	*3 tbsp finely chopped coriander*
2 garlic cloves, crushed	*yoghurt, to serve*
½ tsp chilli powder, or to taste	

❖ Drain the chick-peas and cook in boiling water for 20-30 minutes until just soft.

❖ Dry-fry the seeds together in a heavy-based pan until the aroma rises. Add the oregano and fry for a few more seconds.

❖ Put the seeds, oregano and nuts in a blender and grind to a powder.

❖ Heat the oil in a heavy-based flameproof casserole. Add the onion and gently fry for 10 minutes until translucent. Add the garlic, ground seed mixture and chilli powder. Stir-fry for 2 minutes.

❖ Add the tomatoes, chick-peas, remaining vegetables and the stock. Bring to the boil, season with salt, then cover and simmer for 1 hour.

❖ Check the seasoning, adding more salt or chilli powder if necessary. Stir in the coriander and serve with yogurt.

QUINOA PILAU WITH PEANUT SAUCE

SERVES 4

DRY-ROASTING THE QUINOA BRINGS OUT A NUTTY AROMA AND HELPS KEEP THE GRAINS LIGHT AND SEPARATE WHEN COOKED. THE SWEETNESS OF THE BUTTERNUT SQUASH HELPS BALANCE THE QUINOA'S SLIGHT BITTERNESS.

200 g/7 oz quinoa	*5 tender celery stalks plus leaves, diced finely*
100 g/4 oz French beans	*½ tsp salt*
50 g/2 oz butter	*pepper*
1 bay leaf	*500 ml/18 fl oz Strong Vegetable Stock (page 111)*
½ onion, diced finely	*Peanut Sauce, to serve (page 109)*
75 g/3 oz diced butternut squash (about 1 small squash)	

❖ Wash the quinoa thoroughly until the water becomes clear, then drain in a fine-meshed sieve. Spread out evenly in a roasting tin. Roast in the oven at 170°C/325°F/gas mark 3 for 20 minutes, stirring every 5 minutes until the moisture has evaporated, then every 2-3 minutes until the grains move freely and turn golden.

❖ Plunge the beans in boiling water for 2 minutes. Drain and cut into 2 cm/¾ inch lengths.

❖ Melt the butter in a heavy-based casserole. Add the bay leaf, onion, butternut squash and celery. Simmer for 3-4 minutes, stirring occasionally. Stir in the quinoa and fry for 3-4 minutes. Season with salt and pepper.

❖ Add the boiling stock, cover and simmer over a low heat for 30 minutes or until all the liquid has been absorbed.

❖ Stir in the beans and leave to stand for a few minutes. Serve with the peanut sauce.

RICE BALLS WITH ALFALFA AND LEEKS

SERVES 4 - 6

THE SECRET OF GETTING RICE BALLS TO STICK TOGETHER
IS TO COOK THE RICE IN MORE WATER THAN USUAL, ABOUT
500 ML/18 FL OZ FOR THE QUANTITY HERE, SO THAT IT
BECOMES QUITE GLUTINOUS.

600 g/1¼ lb cooked rice
(250 g/9 oz uncooked weight)
50 g/2 oz leek, shredded and
chopped very finely
75 g/3 oz alfalfa sprouts
3 garlic cloves, crushed
2.5 cm/1 inch piece fresh
ginger root, chopped very finely

4 tbsp tamari (Japanese soy
sauce)
pepper
4 tbsp sesame seeds
4 tbsp plain flour
groundnut oil, for deep frying

❖ Thoroughly mix first 7 ingredients.
❖ With slightly wet hands, form the mixture into about 12 balls, pressing them together firmly. If you still have difficulty making the rice stick, put the mixture in a food processor and blend for 20 seconds.
❖ Roll each ball in the sesame seeds, then in the flour.
❖ Pour about 10 cm/4 inches of oil into a wok or deep pan. Heat to 180°C/350°F or until a cube of bread browns in 30 seconds, then fry the rice balls, a few at a time, for 2-3 minutes until brown and crisp.
❖ Drain on paper towels and serve warm or at room temperature with Spicy Ginger and Sesame Sauce (page 108), Carrot and Coriander Relish (page 109), and Tangy Peanut Sauce (page 106).

PEANUT AND EGG CURRY

SERVES 4

IF THE PEANUTS HAVE SKINS, TOAST THEM IN THE
OVEN FOR 10 MINUTES THEN ROLL IN A TEA TOWEL AND
RUB OFF THE SKINS.

25 g/1 oz dried coconut ribbons
1 tsp coriander seeds
½ tsp cumin seeds
seeds from 6 cardamom pods
2 tbsp sunflower oil
2 onions, sliced
1 garlic clove, crushed
2.5 cm/1 inch piece fresh root
ginger, chopped
½-1 tsp cayenne
½ tsp turmeric
½ tsp salt
400 g/14 oz can chopped
tomatoes

225g/8 oz large, unsalted
peanuts
2 tbsp finely chopped coriander
1 tsp sugar
pepper
300 ml/½ pint Strong Vegetable
Stock (page 111)
2 hard-boiled eggs, halved
1 tbsp lemon juice
coriander leaves, to garnish
Cucumber and Mango Raita, to
serve (page 110)

❖ Toast the coconut ribbons in the oven at 180°C/350°F/gas mark 5 for 3-5 minutes until golden. Dry-fry the coriander, cumin and cardamom seeds in a small heavy pan until the aroma rises.
❖ Grind to a powder the coconut, coriander, cumin and cardamom seeds in a pestle and mortar or coffee grinder.
❖ Heat the oil in a frying pan and gently fry the onions over a low heat for 10 minutes until just coloured.
❖ Add the garlic, ginger, ground spices, cayenne, turmeric and salt. Gently fry for another 5 minutes.
❖ Stir in the tomatoes, peanuts, coriander, sugar, pepper, and stock. Bring to the boil then simmer over a low heat, uncovered, for 30 minutes, adding a little water or stock if the mixture becomes dry.
❖ Carefully stir in the hard-boiled egg halves and lemon juice and simmer for 10 more minutes.
❖ Pour into a serving dish and garnish with coriander.
❖ Serve with plain, boiled rice and Cucumber and Mango Raita.

BLACK AND WHITE CHILLI WITH POLENTA CROSTINI

SERVES 6 - 8

POLENTA

250 g/9 oz cornmeal (polenta)	*1 litre/1¾ pints water*
1¼ tsp salt	*olive oil*

CHILLI

350 g/12 oz black kidney or	*¼-1 tsp chilli powder*
turtle beans, soaked overnight	*2 x 400 g/14 oz cans chopped*
175 g/6 oz haricot beans,	*tomatoes*
soaked overnight	*3 tbsp tomato paste*
1 tsp cumin seeds	*1 tsp sugar*
2 tsp coriander seeds	*1 tsp salt*
2 tsp dried oregano	*600 ml/1 pint Vegetable Stock*
2 tbsp olive oil	*(page 111)*
2 onions, chopped	*3 tbsp chopped coriander (or*
2 garlic cloves, chopped finely	*flat-leafed parsley)*
2 red peppers, cored, deseeded	
and cut into 1.5 cm/½ inch dice	

GARNISH
coriander leaves

❖ Put the polenta, salt and water in a large saucepan and stir thoroughly. Slowly bring to the boil, stirring, then pour into a greased 30.5 x 23 cm/12 x 19 inch roasting tin. Cover with greased foil and bake in the oven at 200°C/400°F/gas mark 6 for at least 1 hour. Allow to cool slightly then turn out and leave to become firm.

❖ When ready to make the crostini, cut the polenta into diamond-shaped slices, brush with olive oil and toast under the grill until lightly browned on both sides.

❖ To make the chilli, drain the beans, put in separate saucepans and cover with fresh water. Boil rapidly for at least 15 minutes then simmer for 30-45 minutes until just tender. Drain and set aside.

❖ Toast the cumin and coriander seeds in a dry pan over a medium heat, shaking the pan so that they do not burn. Add the oregano, toast for 10 seconds, then remove the pan from the heat. Lightly crush the mixture with a pestle and mortar.

❖ Heat the oil in a large saucepan. Add the onion, garlic, red pepper, toasted spice mixture and chilli. Gently fry over a medium heat for 5 minutes until the onion is soft.

❖ Add the chopped tomatoes, tomato paste, sugar, salt, beans and stock. Stir well and bring to the boil. Cover and simmer over a low heat for 45 minutes, stirring occasionally to prevent sticking.

❖ Stir in the coriander and simmer for 5 more minutes.

❖ Garnish with coriander leaves and serve with the polenta crostini.

RICE AND PEAS WITH TOMATO ROUGAIL

SERVES 4

A MAINSTAY OF THE WEST INDIES, REFERRED TO AS RICE AND PEAS IN JAMAICA AND HAITI, EVEN THOUGH THE PEAS ARE IN FACT BEANS. ROUGAIL IS A HIGHLY SPICED WEST INDIAN RELISH TRADITIONALLY SERVED WITH RICE-BASED DISHES.

100 g/4 oz black or red kidney beans, soaked overnight
½ tsp salt
2 tbsp sunflower oil
2 tbsp finely chopped thyme or marjoram
1 small onion, chopped finely

1 small red pepper, deseeded and diced
1 small fresh chilli, deseeded and chopped
1 garlic clove, chopped finely
pepper
225 g/8 oz white rice, washed

COCONUT MILK

350 g/12 oz shredded coconut, fresh or dried
1 litre/1¾ pints hot water or milk and/or liquid from a fresh coconut

TOMATO ROUGAIL

1 small onion, chopped
1 cm/½ inch piece fresh root ginger, chopped
1 fresh red chilli, deseeded and chopped

¼ tsp salt
1 tbsp lemon juice
2 large tomatoes, peeled, deseeded and chopped

GARNISH

15 g/½ oz toasted coconut ribbons
chopped thyme

❖ Rinse and drain the beans. Put them in a saucepan with enough water to cover. Bring to the boil and boil rapidly for 15 minutes then drain again. Cover with fresh water and simmer for about 45-60 minutes until tender, adding salt during the last 10 minutes of cooking time. Drain and set aside.

❖ Put the shredded coconut in a saucepan and add the hot liquid. Cover and simmer over a very low heat for 30 minutes.

❖ Strain through a piece of muslin, twisting the muslin and squeezing the pulp to extract as much juice as possible.

❖ Put all the ingredients for the rougail in a food processor and blend until smooth. Cover and leave to stand at room temperature.

❖ Heat the oil in a large heavy-based saucepan and fry the thyme for 30 seconds. Add the onion and gently fry for 5 minutes until translucent. Add the red pepper and chilli and fry for 3 minutes, then add the garlic and fry for 2 more minutes until the vegetables are soft but not coloured. Season with salt and pepper.

❖ Add the beans and rice and gently fry for 1-2 minutes, stirring until all the rice grains and beans are coated with oil.

❖ Pour the coconut milk over the bean mixture, stir well, bring to the boil, then cover and simmer for about 20 minutes until the liquid is absorbed.

❖ Transfer to a warm serving dish. Fluff with a fork, mixing in the coconut ribbons. Garnish with thyme and serve with the tomato rougail.

CARIBBEAN BLACK BEAN SALAD WITH PALM HEARTS

SERVES 4-6

SOLD IN CANS, PALM HEARTS ARE THE TENDER BUDS OF A
WEST INDIAN PALM TREE. THEY HAVE A FLAVOUR SIMILAR
TO GLOBE ARTICHOKES AND A CRUNCHY TEXTURE.

*175 g/6 oz black kidney or
turtle beans, soaked overnight
400 g/14 oz can palm
hearts, drained
½ red pepper, cored, deseeded
and diced finely*

*2 spring onions, green parts
included, diced finely
1 fresh red or green chilli,
deseeded and sliced finely
3 tbsp finely chopped coriander
or parsley*

DRESSING

*3 tbsp lime juice
grated zest of 1 lime*

*½ tsp sugar
4 tbsp olive oil*

❖ Drain and rinse the beans. Cover with water and boil
rapidly for 15 minutes, then drain, rinse and cover with
fresh water. Simmer for 20-30 minutes until just tender,
adding salt during the last 10 minutes of cooking time.
Drain the beans again and put in a serving bowl.

❖ Combine the dressing ingredients, season and whisk
until thick. Pour it over the beans while they are still warm,
mixing well. Leave the beans to cool.

❖ Cut the palm hearts crossways into 1 cm/½ inch diagonal
slices. Add to the beans with the remaining ingredients.

❖ Toss well, then leave to stand at room temperature for at
least 1 hour before serving.

RICE SALAD WITH MANGETOUT AND LEMON GRASS

SERVES 4

AN ESSENTIAL FLAVOURING IN SOUTH EAST ASIAN
COOKERY, LEMON GRASS HAS A SUBTLE BUT DISTINCTIVE
FRAGRANCE. IF YOU'RE LUCKY ENOUGH TO FIND LARGE
FRESH LEMON GRASS STALKS, IT'S WORTH BUYING SOME TO
FREEZE, OR THEY WILL KEEP FOR TWO WEEKS IN THE SALAD
DRAWER OF THE REFRIGERATOR.

*2 long lemon grass stalks
150 g/5 oz long-grain rice
½ tsp salt
125 ml/4 fl oz Vegetable Stock
(page 110)
1 garlic clove, crushed
pinch ground cumin
½ dried red chilli, deseeded
and crumbled*

*2 tbsp lime juice
3 tbsp olive oil
salt and pepper
100 g/4 oz mangetout or sugar
snap peas, trimmed
2 spring onions, green parts
included, sliced finely
40 g/1½ oz unsalted peanuts,
roasted*

❖ Remove and discard the tough outer stalks of the lemon
grass. Chop the remaining tender stalks very finely.

❖ Wash the rice in several changes of water until the water
becomes clear. Put in a small saucepan with enough water
to cover by 2.5 cm/1 inch. Add the salt and half the lemon
grass. Bring to the boil then cover and simmer over a low
heat for 20 minutes until the water is absorbed.

❖ Meanwhile, put the remaining lemon grass in a small
saucepan with the stock and simmer for 10 minutes. Pour
into a blender with the garlic, cumin, chilli, lime juice,
olive oil, salt and pepper, and purée until smooth.

❖ Put the rice in a shallow serving dish and pour the
blended lemon grass mixture over it while the rice is still
warm. Fluff gently with a fork and leave to cool.

❖ Steam the mangetout over boiling water for 2 minutes.
Drain under cold running water and pat dry with paper
towels. Slice into 2 cm/¾ inch pieces and add to the rice.

❖ Stir in the spring onions and roasted peanuts. Leave to
stand for 1 hour at room temperature before serving.

STIR-FRIED BROWN RICE WITH SHIITAKE MUSHROOMS AND SEA VEGETABLES

SERVES 4

SEA VEGETABLES ARE HIGHLY VALUED IN JAPAN. TRY THE MILDER ONES, ARAME OR HIZIKI, TO START WITH.

7.5 g/¼ oz arame or hiziki

2 tbsp tamari (Japanese soy sauce)

1 tbsp umeboshi vinegar (or white wine vinegar)

1 tsp wasabi powder (optional)

2 tbsp sunflower oil

2 tsp dark sesame oil

3 garlic cloves, chopped finely

2.5 cm/ 1 inch piece fresh ginger root, chopped very finely

75 g/ 3 oz yellow pepper, cut into matchstick strips

75 g/3 oz shiitake mushrooms, sliced very finely

50 g/2 oz leek (green and white parts), cut into matchstick strips

275 g/10 oz cooked brown rice (about 150 g/5 oz dry weight)

❖ Rinse and soak the arame in cold water for at least 1 hour. Drain and reserve the soaking water.

❖ Combine the tamari and umeboshi in a small bowl then stir in the wasabi powder if using.

❖ Heat the oils in a wok or frying pan. Add the garlic and ginger and stir-fry over a high heat for 10 seconds. Add the yellow pepper, mushrooms, leek, arame and 2 tablespoons of the arame soaking water. Stir-fry for about 2 minutes then transfer to a bowl and keep warm.

❖ Add the rice to the wok, sprinkle with 3 tablespoons of arame soaking water and stir-fry for 2 minutes until heated through. Stir in the tamari mixture.

❖ Return the vegetables to the pan and stir until heated through.

TOFU AND CASHEW NUT STIR-FRY

SERVES 4

WRAP THE TOFU IN SEVERAL LAYERS OF PAPER TOWEL AND LEAVE WITH A WEIGHT ON TOP TO DRAIN FOR 30 MINUTES. IT SHOULD BE AS DRY AS POSSIBLE.

400 g/14 oz firm tofu, drained and pressed dry

4 tbsp hoisin sauce

1 tbsp dry sherry

1 tbsp soy sauce

½ tsp salt

pepper

4-5 spring onions

3 tbsp groundnut oil

3 garlic cloves, chopped finely

3 slices fresh ginger root, chopped finely

2 fresh chillies, deseeded and sliced finely

150 g/5 oz shiitake mushrooms, sliced thinly

75 g/3 oz roasted, unsalted cashew nuts

2 tsp dark sesame oil

❖ Cut the tofu in half horizontally and then into 1 cm/ ½ inch cubes. Mix together the hoisin sauce, sherry, soy sauce, salt and pepper in a bowl.

❖ Cut the spring onions into 3, separating the white and green parts. Cut each piece lengthways into shreds.

❖ Heat 2 tablespoons of the groundnut oil in a wok or frying pan until almost smoking. Add two-thirds of the garlic and ginger and stir-fry for 30 seconds.

❖ Add the chillis, white part of the spring onions and the mushrooms. Stir-fry for 2 minutes then set aside.

❖ Heat the remaining oil over a high heat and stir-fry the remaining garlic and ginger for a few seconds.

❖ Add the tofu with the hoisin sauce mixture and stir-fry over a medium heat for 3 minutes until heated through.

❖ Return the mushroom mixture to the pan and toss in the sauce until well coated.

❖ Stir in the cashew nuts and green spring onion. Sprinkle with sesame oil and serve immediately.

FALAFEL WITH MINTED YOGURT SAUCE

SERVES 4-6

COATING THE FALAFEL WITH EGG YOLK IS NOT
STRICTLY AUTHENTIC, BUT IT HELPS PREVENT THE
CHICK-PEAS FROM FALLING APART.

200 g/7 oz chick-peas or dried	*2 tbsp flour*
broad beans, soaked overnight	*¼ tsp baking powder*
2 tsp coriander seeds	*salt and cayenne pepper*
1 tsp cumin seeds	*beaten egg yolk*
1 onion, grated	*flour for dusting*
2 garlic cloves, crushed	*groundnut oil, for frying*
4 tbsp finely chopped coriander	*Minted Yogurt Sauce*
or parsley	*(page 107), to serve*
4 tbsp lemon juice	

❖ Drain and rinse the chick-peas. Put in a large saucepan of water. Bring to the boil and simmer for 20-30 minutes until soft. Add salt in the last 10 minutes of cooking time.

❖ Dry-fry the spices in a small, heavy pan until the aroma rises. Then crush in a mortar.

❖ Drain the chick-peas and purée in a food processor with the spices and remaining ingredients until smooth. Chill the mixture for at least 1 hour.

❖ Form into flattish cakes, about 4 cm/1½ inches in diameter, pressing the mixture together firmly. Dip in beaten egg yolk and roll in flour. Chill for 15 minutes.

❖ Pour about 10 cm/4 inches of oil into a deep pan. Heat to 180°C/350°F or until a cube of bread browns in 30 seconds. Fry the falafel for about 3 minutes until golden brown. Drain on paper towels.

❖ Stuff into warmed pitta bread pockets with a spoonful of yogurt sauce, sliced onions, shredded lettuce and lemon wedges.

LENTIL AND CHERRY TOMATO SALAD WITH GINGER DRESSING

SERVES 4

PUY LENTILS ARE BEST FOR THIS DISH AS THEY HAVE A
ROBUST, EARTHY FLAVOUR. ALLOW THE SALAD TO STAND AT
ROOM TEMPERATURE FOR AN HOUR OR TWO.

200 g/7 oz Puy lentils, rinsed	*100 g/4 oz cherry tomatoes*
coarse sea salt	*1 tbsp toasted sesame seeds*
pepper	*120 ml/4 fl oz yogurt or double*
3 spring onions	*cream*

DRESSING

5 cm/2 inch piece fresh root	*1½ tsp sugar*
ginger, crushed in a garlic press	*salt and pepper*
1 tbsp lime or lemon juice	*4 tbsp olive oil*
1 garlic clove, crushed	*1 tsp dark sesame oil*

❖ Whisk together all the dressing ingredients in the order listed and set aside.

❖ Put the lentils in a saucepan with 600 ml/1 pint of water. Bring to the boil and simmer for 15 minutes until just tender. Drain and transfer to a serving dish.

❖ Pour half the dressing over the lentils while they are still warm. Season generously with coarse sea salt and freshly ground pepper. Leave to cool.

❖ Cut the spring onions, green parts included, into 3 cm/1¼ inch pieces. Cut the pieces lengthways into shreds.

❖ Stir all but 1 tablespoon of the onions into the lentils. Halve the tomatoes and add with the sesame seeds.

❖ Mix the remaining dressing with the yogurt and stir into the lentils. Garnish with the remaining onions.

CORIANDER DHAL WITH CARAMELISED ONION RINGS

SERVES 4

TRADITIONALLY USED IN PEASE PUDDING, A DISH
FROM NORTHERN ENGLAND, YELLOW SPLIT PEAS HAVE A
WARM EARTHY FLAVOUR WHICH COMBINES WELL WITH
SPICES. ALTHOUGH NOT STRICTLY NECESSARY, SOAKING
FOR AN HOUR OR TWO BEFOREHAND WILL HELP THE PEAS
BREAK DOWN TO A PUREE.

225 g/8 oz yellow split peas, rinsed	*½ tsp mustard seeds*
1 litre/1¾ pints water	*4 garlic cloves, crushed*
10 black peppercorns	*2.5 cm/1 inch piece fresh root ginger, chopped finely*
½ tsp coriander seeds	*½ tsp turmeric*
3 cloves	*½ tsp chilli powder*
seeds from 2 cardamom pods	*2 tbsp lemon juice*
2 onions	*1 tsp salt*
2 tbsp sunflower oil	*3 tbsp finely chopped coriander*
25 g/1 oz butter	

GARNISH
coriander leaves

❖ Put the peas in a saucepan with the water. Bring to the boil and simmer for 30 minutes until most of the liquid is absorbed and the peas are very soft.
❖ Crush the peppercorns, coriander seeds, cloves and cardamom seeds in a mortar and set aside.
❖ Chop 1 of the onions very finely and set aside. Cut the other onion into 5 mm/¼ inch thick slices. Keep the rings in place by inserting 2 or 3 wooden cocktail sticks from the outside to the centre. Brush both sides with some of the oil and place under a very hot grill for 5-7 minutes each side until blackened round the edges.
❖ Heat the butter and remaining oil in a pan and fry the mustard seeds until they begin to pop. Add the chopped onion and gently fry for 5-7 minutes until translucent.
❖ Add the garlic and ginger and fry for another 2-3 minutes then stir in the turmeric, chilli powder and the crushed spices. Stir-fry for 2 minutes.
❖ Add the peas, stir in the lemon juice, salt and chopped coriander and simmer for a few minutes over a low heat. Add a little water if the mixture becomes dry.
❖ Transfer to a heated serving dish and top with the onion rings, removing the cocktail sticks first. Garnish with coriander leaves and serve with yogurt.

WILD RICE AND HAZELNUT SALAD

SERVES 4

A ROBUST SALAD, WARMLY
FLAVOURED WITH ORANGE, GINGER AND THYME.

175 g/6 oz wild rice, rinsed	*350 g/12 oz young broad beans,*
1 bay leaf	*shelled (or 75 g/3 oz frozen)*
1 strip orange zest	*125 g/4 oz fine French beans*
salt	*pepper*
450 ml/16 fl oz water	*bitter and pungent green*
2 tbsp finely chopped thyme	*leaves e.g. escarole, rocket,*
40 g/1½ oz shelled hazelnuts	*watercress, to serve*

❖ Place the rice in a saucepan with the bay leaf, orange zest, ½ teaspoon salt and the water. Bring to the boil, then simmer, covered, for 35-40 minutes until tender. The rice should still be quite chewy and not mushy. Drain, discarding the bay leaf and orange zest, and mix with the dressing and thyme while still warm.

❖ Toast the hazelnuts in the oven at 180°C/350°F/gas mark 4 for 10 minutes. Remove the skins by rolling in a clean, dry tea towel. Chop roughly and add to the rice.

❖ Steam the broad and French beans together over boiling water for 3-4 minutes until barely tender. Rinse under cold water and pat dry with paper towels. Cut the French beans into 2.5 cm/1 inch lengths. Stir the beans into the rice.

❖ Add salt and freshly ground pepper to taste. Leave to stand at room temperature to allow the flavours to develop.

❖ Arrange a bed of salad leaves on 4 serving plates and pile the rice in the centre.

CHESTNUT, CELERY AND ORANGE SOUP

SERVES 4

A ZESTY SOUP WITH HIDDEN DEPTHS OF FLAVOUR. USE
EITHER 700 G/1½ LB FRESH CHESTNUTS, PEELED AND
HUSKED; 350 G/12 OZ FROZEN CHESTNUTS; OR 175 G/6 OZ
DRIED CHESTNUTS, SOAKED OVERNIGHT THEN SIMMERED
FOR 1½ HOURS.

50 g/2 oz butter	*½ tsp ground ginger*
1 onion, chopped	*850 ml/1½ pints Vegetable*
4 sticks celery, chopped	*Stock (page 111)*
350 g/12 oz prepared chestnuts	*100 ml/3½ fl oz orange juice*
2 x 5 cm/2 inch slithers of	*4 tbsp double cream and*
orange zest	*chopped celery leaves or lovage,*
½ tsp salt	*to garnish*
1/2 tsp freshly ground black	
pepper	

❖ Melt the butter in a saucepan and add the onion and celery. Cover and sweat together for about 5 minutes.

❖ Add the chestnuts and all the remaining ingredients except the orange juice. Cover and simmer for 30 minutes.

❖ Pour into a food processor and blend until smooth. Return to the pan and add the orange juice. Reheat gently and pour into bowls.

❖ Add a swirl of cream to each bowl and sprinkle with chopped celery leaves or lovage.

BLACK BEAN SOUP WITH YOGURT

SERVES 4

A THICK, FILLING SOUP WITH EXCITING FLAVOURS. START
MAKING IT THE DAY BEFORE YOU PLAN TO SERVE IT.

*175 g/6 oz black kidney beans,
soaked overnight*
3 tbsp olive oil
2 bay leaves
2 sprigs thyme
2 small sprigs rosemary
1 onion, chopped
*4 garlic cloves, peeled and left
whole*
2 celery stalks, chopped

1 small leek, chopped
2 carrots, chopped
*700 ml/1½ pints Vegetable
Stock (page 111)*
*2 tsp whole black peppercorns,
crushed*
*2 tsp coriander seeds, toasted
and crushed*
½ tsp salt
1 tbsp lemon juice

GARNISH

plain yogurt | *finely chopped coriander*

❖ Drain the beans and rinse well. Put in a saucepan with enough water to cover. Bring to the boil and boil rapidly for 15 minutes, then drain and rinse.

❖ Heat the oil in a large, heavy-based pan. Add the herbs and cook for 30 seconds to flavour the oil. Add the onion and gently fry for 5 minutes until translucent. Add the garlic, celery, leek, and carrots. Cover and sweat for 10 minutes.

❖ Add the beans, stock, peppercorns and coriander seeds. Bring to the boil, then simmer slowly, covered, for 1 hour until the beans are soft, stirring occasionally.

❖ Purée thoroughly in a food processor and reheat. Season to taste with salt and add the lemon juice.

❖ Serve in large bowls, swirl in a spoonful of yogurt and sprinkle with chopped fresh coriander.

HAZELNUT AND WARM JERUSALEM ARTICHOKE SALAD

SERVES 4

A RICHLY FLAVOURED AUTUMN SALAD. THE EARTHY TASTE
OF THE ARTICHOKES COMBINES WELL WITH THE SWEETNESS
OF THE HAZELNUTS. STEAMING CONSERVES THE FLAVOUR
AND HELPS PREVENT THE SLICES FROM BREAKING UP.

75 g/3 oz shelled hazelnuts
450 g/1 lb Jerusalem artichokes
1 lemon
100 g/4 oz fine French beans
2 tbsp hazelnut oil

*3 tbsp finely chopped parsley
or chervil*
coarse sea salt
pepper

❖ Roast the hazelnuts at 180°C/350°F/gas mark 4 for 8-10 minutes. Rub off the skins in a cloth then chop roughly. Squeeze the juice from half the lemon into a bowl of cold water.

❖ Peel the artichokes, removing any knobbly bits, and cut into 5 mm/¼ inch thick slices, dropping them into the acidulated water as you work.

❖ Trim the beans and cut into 2 cm/¾ inch lengths.

❖ Drain the artichokes and steam with the beans over boiling water for 4-5 minutes until only just tender.

❖ Put into a serving bowl. Sprinkle with the oil and 1 tablespoon of lemon juice and gently toss until all the slices are coated.

❖ Add the hazelnuts and parsley or chervil. Season generously with coarse sea salt and a few twists of the pepper grinder. Toss gently again and serve while still warm.

AUTUMN STIR-FRY OF CHESTNUTS AND MUSHROOMS

SERVES 4

FRESHLY GATHERED CHESTNUTS AND MUSHROOMS MAKE THIS A MAGIC DISH FOR AN AUTUMN SUPPER. BUT IT'S STILL WORTH MAKING WITH CULTIVATED MUSHROOMS AND FROZEN OR DRIED CHESTNUTS. IF USING DRIED CHESTNUTS, SOAK OVERNIGHT, SIMMER FOR 1 1/2 HOURS IN WATER, THEN DRAIN AND FOLLOW THE RECIPE.

175 ml/6 fl oz Vegetable Stock (page 111)
500 g/18 oz fresh chestnuts, peeled and husked, or 100 g/ 4 oz dried, cooked as above, or 200g/7 oz frozen chestnuts
4 tbsp olive oil

225 g/8 oz large mushrooms
2 garlic cloves, chopped very finely
coarse sea salt
pepper
5 tbsp finely chopped parsley

❖ Bring the stock to the boil and add the chestnuts. Bring back to the boil and simmer rapidly for 5-7 minutes. Drain the chestnuts, reserving the stock, and cut each one in half. Boil the stock rapidly until reduced by half, then reserve.

❖ Heat the oil in a frying pan, add the mushrooms and stir-fry for 5 minutes. Add the chestnuts and garlic and fry for another 2-3 minutes.

❖ Add the reduced stock, season generously with coarse sea salt and freshly ground pepper and stir in the parsley. Simmer for another minute or two and serve.

ROASTED BUCKWHEAT WITH KOHLRABI

SERVES 4

USE ROASTED BUCKWHEAT (KASHA) AS IT HAS A BETTER FLAVOUR THAN THE RAW VARIETY. COATING THE BUCKWHEAT WITH EGG KEEPS THE GRAINS SEPARATE AND PREVENTS THEM FROM BECOMING MUSHY.

175 g/6 oz roasted buckwheat
1 egg, beaten
3-4 small kohlrabi (about 450g/ 1 lb)
knob of butter
2 tbsp finely chopped parsley

1 tbsp finely chopped dill
1 tsp fennel seeds, toasted and crushed
salt and pepper
150 ml/¼ pint soured cream
2 tbsp lemon juice

GARNISH
dill leaves | *paprika*

❖ Put the buckwheat in a saucepan with the beaten egg. Stir until all the grains are coated. Place over a medium heat and stir for about 1 minute until the grains are dry and separate. Break up any lumps with a fork. Add enough boiling water to cover by 1 cm/½ inch. Add salt and simmer, uncovered, for about 15 minutes until all the liquid has been absorbed. Cover and keep warm.

❖ Meanwhile, peel the kohlrabi and cut into 5 mm/¼ inch slices. Cut each slice into 4. Simmer in salted water for 4-5 minutes until just tender.

❖ Drain the kohlrabi and return to the pan. Add the butter, parsley, dill and fennel seeds and season generously with salt and pepper. Gently fry for 1-2 minutes then stir in the soured cream and lemon juice, and heat through.

❖ Transfer the buckwheat to a warmed serving dish and top with the kohlrabi mixture. Sprinkle with paprika and garnish with dill leaves.

RED CABBAGE WITH A CRISP NUT STUFFING

SERVES 4-6

A DISH OF VIBRANT COLOUR AND CRUNCHY TEXTURE - PERFECT FOR A WINTER SUPPER. IT MAKES A CHANGE FROM THE USUAL WAY OF COOKING RED CABBAGE WITH VINEGAR, APPLES AND ONIONS.

1 red cabbage (about 1 kg/ 2¼ lb)
4 tbsp olive oil
50g/2 oz butter
100 g/4 oz wholemeal breadcrumbs
175 g/6 oz chopped mixed nuts (Brazil nuts, cashews, walnuts, peanuts)
1 onion, chopped finely

100 g/4 oz mushrooms, sliced thinly
3 garlic cloves, chopped finely
1 tbsp dried herbes de Provence or mixed herbs
grated zest of ½ lemon
½ tsp salt
pepper
300 ml/½ pint Vegetable Stock (page 111)

TO SERVE
Roasted Red Pepper Sauce (page 106) or Tomato Sauce (page 108)

❖ Cut off 4 cm/1½ inches from the base of the cabbage and carefully peel away 6-8 outer leaves. Plunge the leaves into a large saucepan of boiling water for 2-3 minutes. Drain under cold running water and pat dry with paper towels. Using a small, sharp knife, shave away some of the base of the thick stalk so that the leaves are easier to bend.

❖ Cut the centre of the cabbage in half. Discard one piece for use in another dish. Slice the remaining cabbage lengthways into 4 and cut out the thick central stalk. Cut the cabbage crossways into shreds.

❖ To make the stuffing, heat 1 tablespoon of the oil and half the butter in a frying pan. Fry the breadcrumbs and nuts together for 3-4 minutes until the crumbs are crisp. Put the mixture in a bowl and wipe out the pan.

❖ Heat the remaining oil and 15 g/½ oz of the butter and gently fry the onion for a few minutes until translucent. Add the mushrooms and shredded cabbage and fry over a medium heat for 5 minutes. Stir in the garlic and herbs and fry for another 2 minutes. Add to the nut mixture in the bowl.

❖ Stir in the lemon zest, salt, a generous amount of freshly ground pepper and 150 ml/¼ pint of the stock.

❖ Arrange the leaves around the edge of a shallow, oven-proof dish, about 22 cm/8½ inches in diameter, overlapping them so that there are no gaps. Pile the stuffing in the centre, dot with the remaining butter and fold over the tops of the leaves. Pour the remaining stock round the outside of the leaves.

❖ Tightly cover the dish with a double thickness of foil. Bake for 45 minutes at 180°C/350°F/gas mark 4. Serve in wedges with the sauce.

CHICK-PEA AND AUBERGINE DIP

SERVES 4

TO EXTRACT MAXIMUM JUICE FROM THE LIME,
ROLL IT ON A HARD SURFACE BEFORE SQUEEZING.

2 small aubergines	*2 tbsp lime juice*
75 g/3 oz chick-peas, soaked	*1 garlic clove, crushed*
overnight	*2 tbsp olive oil*
¼ tsp salt	*pinch of cayenne*
6 tbsp Greek yogurt	*black olives and cayenne, to*
grated zest of ½ lime	*garnish*

❖ Grill the aubergines for 15-20 minutes, turning occasionally, until charred. Allow to cool slightly then remove the skin. Squeeze out the bitter juices then leave to drain.
❖ Put the chick-peas in a large saucepan of water. Bring to the boil and simmer for about 20 minutes until soft. Add salt during the last 10 minutes of cooking time.
❖ Drain and purée with the aubergines and remaining ingredients until smooth.
❖ Transfer to a serving bowl and garnish.

YELLOW SPLIT PEA AND WALNUT PUREE

SERVES 4

A QUICKLY MADE DIP. SERVE IT WITH
BLUE CORN TORTILLA CHIPS OR WARM PITTA BREAD.

150 g/5 oz yellow split peas,	*2 spring onions, green part*
rinsed and drained	*included, chopped*
40 g/1½ oz shelled walnuts,	*1 tbsp lemon juice*
chopped roughly	*1 tbsp olive oil*
100 ml/4fl oz fromage frais or	*salt and pepper*
Greek yogurt	*walnut pieces and chopped*
1 garlic clove, crushed	*spring onion tops, to garnish*

❖ Put the peas in a saucepan with enough water to cover by 2.5 cm/1 inch. Bring to the boil then simmer, stirring occasionally, for 20-25 minutes until the liquid is absorbed and the peas are soft.
❖ Purée in a food processor with all the remaining ingredients until smooth, adding more lemon juice or salt and pepper if necessary.
❖ Transfer to a serving bowl and garnish with a few walnut pieces and chopped spring onion tops.

LENTIL, MINT AND LEMON DIP

SERVES 4

LENTILS DE PUY HAVE THE BEST FLAVOUR BUT YOU
CAN USE ORDINARY BROWN OR GREEN LENTILS INSTEAD.

100 g/4 oz Puy lentils, soaked	*grated zest of 1 lemon*
overnight	*3 tbsp lemon juice*
1 tsp cumin seeds, toasted and	*3 tbsp olive oil*
crushed	*4 tbsp finely chopped mint*
1 garlic clove, crushed	*salt and pepper*

❖ Drain the soaked lentils and rinse. Put them in a saucepan with 300 ml/½ pint water. Bring to the boil, then simmer for 5 minutes until soft. Drain again.
❖ Put the lentils in a food processor with the remaining ingredients and process until smooth. Add more lemon juice, salt and pepper if necessary.
❖ Transfer to a serving bowl and garnish with a twist of lemon and a mint sprig.

PASTA, PASTRY, PANCAKES AND BREAD

Various types of dough can be made from flour and water or eggs. The recipes in this chapter mainly use wheat flour, although some use chick-pea flour, rice flour, cornmeal or polenta. These all-time staples, combined with vegetables, pulses or dairy products, create satisfying dishes which form the basis of countless vegetarian meals.

Pasta is one of the most comforting of foods – easily made and cooked. There's nothing to beat home-made pasta, using flour moistened with eggs and a little oil, kneaded until elastic, then rolled out. Of the commercial dried pastas, I find the best brands are Italian. Cook pasta in plenty of boiling water – about 5 litres/8 pints for every 450 g/1 lb of pasta. Cooking times can only be approximate so you need to test to see if it's ready. The pasta should be tender but still with some bite to it.

Meltingly crisp golden pastry makes a very appealing foil to a variety of fillings – colourful chunks of grilled or stir-fried vegetables, or puffy, egg-based custards seasoned with herbs. Pastry dishes are best accompanied by a crisp salad or plainly cooked vegetables of a contrasting type or colour to the filling.

Pancakes and tortillas are great for mopping up sauces and dips, or they can be filled with tasty well-seasoned morsels of freshly cooked food or leftovers. No meal is complete without bread. Any doubts you have about making your own will soon disappear once you experience the satisfaction of transforming what can be a sticky mess into a silky smooth elastic dough – and eating the results.

CONTENTS

NOODLES WITH GRILLED MARINATED VEGETABLES

SERVES 4

THIS MARINADE IS RATHER LIKE A
PESTO SAUCE WITH ORIENTAL UNDERTONES.

2 small red onions, unpeeled
2 heads of purple 'wet' garlic
4 small courgettes
2 small plump heads of chicory

1 aubergine
1 large yellow pepper, deseeded
olive oil for brushing
100 g/4 oz egg vermicelli

MARINADE

handful of torn basil leaves
handful of fennel fronds
handful of coriander, trimmed
and chopped roughly
2.5 cm/1 inch piece fresh ginger
root, chopped finely
2 large garlic cloves, chopped

1 fresh chilli, deseeded and
chopped
juice and finely grated zest of 1
lime
8 tbsp olive oil
50 g/2 oz peanuts, toasted
1 tsp muscovado sugar
½ tsp salt

❖ Purée the marinade ingredients in a blender until smooth.

❖ Cut the onions and garlic in half crossways and the courgettes and chicory lengthways. Cut the yellow pepper into quarters and slice the aubergine lengthways.

❖ Place the vegetables in a single layer in a dish. Brush with the marinade and sprinkle with olive oil. Cover and marinate for at least 2 hours, preferably overnight.

❖ Remove the vegetables, scraping off and reserving the marinade, and place on a rack over medium-hot coals or under a preheated grill. Grill for 10-15 minutes, brushing with oil and turning, until tender and beginning to blacken.

❖ Meanwhile, cook the vermicelli. Drain, return to the pan and toss with the reserved marinade. Arrange a nest of vermicelli on 4 plates and top with a selection of grilled vegetables.

SPICED ONION BREAD

MAKES 1 LOAF

ADAPTED FROM AN ETHIOPIAN RECIPE, A SLICE OF THIS
ROBUSTLY FLAVOURED LOAF IS ALMOST A MEAL IN ITSELF.
DELICIOUS STILL WARM FROM THE OVEN AND THICKLY
SPREAD WITH UNSALTED BUTTER.

15 g/½ oz fresh yeast
1 tsp brown sugar
225 ml/8 fl oz tepid water
1 small onion, chopped finely
1 garlic clove, chopped finely
75 g/3 oz butter
2 tsp cumin seeds
2 tsp coriander seeds
1 tsp fenugreek seeds

1 tsp sesame seeds
1½ tsp salt
¾ tsp coarsely ground black
pepper
¼ tsp cayenne
2 tsp grated fresh ginger root
450 g/1 lb strong white flour
melted butter, to glaze

❖ Mix the yeast, sugar and water until frothy. Fry the onion and garlic in 25 g/1 oz of the butter until the onion is translucent. Dry-fry the seeds for a few minutes then grind to a powder.

❖ Melt the remaining butter. Stir in the seeds, ginger and onion. Add 100 g/4 oz flour. Whisk in the yeast liquid. Cover and leave in a warm place for 1 hour.

❖ Add the remaining flour and knead for 15 minutes. Place in an oiled bowl, cover and leave in a warm place for 1-2 hours until doubled in size. Knock back and form into a loaf shape. Place on a floured baking sheet and cut a cross in the centre. Leave to rise for 20 minutes.

❖ Bake at 180°C/350°F/gas mark 4 for 50-60 minutes until the bottom sounds hollow when tapped. Brush with melted butter while still warm.

FUSILLI WITH CORIANDER PESTO

SERVES 4

CORIANDER INSTEAD OF BASIL GIVES A NEW SLANT TO PESTO. PECORINO SARDO CHEESE IS LESS SALTY THAN THE MORE WIDELY AVAILABLE ROMANO TYPE. IF YOU USE ROMANO, REDUCE THE QUANTITY TO TASTE.

50 g/2 oz trimmed coriander
4 tbsp extra virgin olive oil
1 garlic clove, chopped finely
25 g/1 oz pine kernels, toasted
2 tsp lime juice
coarse sea salt
black pepper

25 g/1 oz freshly grated Parmesan
1½ tbsp finely grated pecorino sardo cheese
225 g/8 oz young French beans, trimmed
250 g/9 oz fusilli

❖ Put the coriander, olive oil, garlic, pine kernels and lime juice in a food processor with a generous pinch of sea salt and several grindings of black pepper. Blend until smooth.
❖ Transfer to a bowl and whisk in the cheeses.
❖ Plunge the beans into boiling salted water for 3 minutes. Drain, chop into 2.5 cm/1 inch lengths and keep warm.
❖ Boil the fusilli in salted water until just tender. Drain and toss with the beans and coriander pesto. Serve immediately with a cherry tomato salad.

ORIENTAL NOODLE SALAD WITH CUCUMBER, MUSHROOMS AND SEA VEGETABLES

SERVES 6

A DRAMATIC SALAD WITH JUST A HINT OF SEA VEGETABLE. IT'S IMPORTANT TO USE TAMARI (JAPANESE SOY SAUCE) AS ORDINARY SOY SAUCE IS TOO HARSH. YOU CAN BUY TAMARI AND SEA VEGETABLES FROM GOOD HEALTHFOOD STORES.

18 yellow oyster mushrooms
3 tbsp vegetable oil
25g/1 oz dried arame (sea vegetable), soaked for 2 hours
2 tbsp tamari

150 g/5 oz Chinese cellophane rice noodles
1 tbsp dark sesame oil
½ cucumber cut into matchstick strips

DRESSING

4 tbsp toasted sesame seeds
2 tbsp tamari
1 tbsp sunflower oil
½ tsp dark sesame oil

2 tsp rice vinegar
1½ tsp sugar
½ tsp salt
⅛ tsp pepper

❖ Gently fry the mushrooms in 2 tablespoons of the oil for 5 minutes. Drain on paper towels and leave to cool.
❖ Drain the arame, reserving the soaking water, and add to the pan with the remaining oil. Stir-fry for 5 minutes. Add the tamari and all but 4 tablespoons of soaking water. Simmer until the liquid has almost evaporated. Spread out on a plate to cool.
❖ Cook the noodles as directed on the packet. Rinse and drain thoroughly then toss in a bowl with the sesame oil.
❖ To make the dressing, grind 3 tablespoons of the sesame seeds to a powder in a blender. Add to the remaining ingredients with the arame soaking water. Whisk until thick.
❖ Divide the noodles between 6 plates, spreading them out in a circle. Make a circle of arame in the centre then pour some dressing over the arame. Top with a pile of cucumber strips and place 3 mushrooms round the edge. Sprinkle with the whole sesame seeds and serve.

HERBED CORNMEAL TARTLETS WITH ASPARAGUS AND MUSHROOMS

SERVES 8

THE POLENTA GIVES THE PASTRY A PLEASANTLY GRITTY TEXTURE WHICH CONTRASTS WELL WITH THE VEGETABLES. SAVE TIME AND WASHING UP BY STEAMING THE VEGETABLES TOGETHER. PUT THE ASPARAGUS AT THE BOTTOM OF THE STEAMER BASKET, THEN THE BABY CORN, WITH THE CARROTS ON TOP.

DOUGH

150 g/5 oz self-raising flour	*2 tbsp finely chopped mixed*
100 g/4 oz polenta or cornmeal	*herbs e.g. thyme, oregano,*
salt	*lovage, hyssop, savory*
cayenne	*100 g/4 oz butter*
	4 tbsp cold water

FILLING

16 asparagus spears, stalks	*salt and pepper*
trimmed and peeled	*225 ml/8 fl oz Vegetable Stock*
8 baby sweetcorn ears	*(page 111)*
50 g/2 oz thinly sliced carrot	*2 tsp cornflour, blended to a*
200 g/7 oz small mushrooms,	*paste with a little stock*
sliced thinly	*2 tbsp finely chopped chives*
1 tbsp sunflower oil	*1½ tsp lemon juice*

❖ Sift the flour and polenta into a mixing bowl with a pinch of salt and cayenne. Add the herbs then rub in the butter until the mixture resembles fine breadcrumbs. Stir in the water to form a smooth dough. Cover with cling-film and chill for 30 minutes.

❖ Roll out the dough to a 3 mm/¼ inch thickness. Cut out 8 x 12.5 cm/5 inch circles, using the trimmings to make up the required amount. Use to line 8 fluted 100 cm/4 inch diameter greased tart tins, pressing the dough well into the edges. Place on a baking sheet and bake at 200°C/400°F/gas mark 6 for 20 minutes until slightly golden.

❖ Meanwhile, steam the asparagus, baby sweetcorn and carrots over boiling water for 5 minutes until only just tender. Reserve the asparagus tips as a garnish and cut the stalks and the sweetcorn into 1 cm/½ inch slices.

❖ Stir-fry the mushrooms in the oil for 5 minutes, seasoning with salt and pepper.

❖ Add the stock and bring to the boil. Add the cornflour and stir until thickened. Add the chives and lemon juice then gently stir in the asparagus stalks, sweetcorn and carrots. Simmer for 1 minute to heat through. Check the seasoning.

❖ Spoon the mixture into the tartlet cases and garnish with the reserved asparagus tips. Serve immediately.

ITALIAN VEGETABLE PIES

SERVES 8

SWISS CHARD STEMS ARE A VEGETABLE IN THEIR OWN RIGHT. CUT THEM FROM THE LEAVES AND STIR-FRY WITH THE BROAD BEANS. IF YOU CAN'T GET HOLD OF CHARD, USE HALF THE QUANTITY OF SPINACH WITH ABOUT 450 G/1 LB CHOPPED CELERY OR ASPARAGUS STEMS.

PASTRY

350 g/12 oz plain flour	2 tbsp olive oil
1½ tsp salt	9 tbsp cold water
1 egg	beaten egg yolk, to glaze

FILLING

900 g/2 lb Swiss chard	2 tbsp finely chopped flat-leafed
1 tbsp olive oil	parsley
50 g butter	2 tbsp finely chopped savory
1 garlic clove, chopped finely	or thyme
2 shallots, chopped finely	salt and pepper
350 g/12 oz frozen broad beans,	2 eggs , beaten
defrosted	4 tbsp freshly grated Parmesan

❖ Sift the flour and salt into a large bowl. Make a well in the centre and add the egg, oil and water. Mix with a wooden spoon, gradually drawing in the flour. Knead briefly to form a smooth dough. Wrap in cling-film and chill for at least 1 hour.

❖ Cook the chard leaves in a very little salted water for 5 minutes. Drain, and when cool enough to handle, squeeze out as much moisture as possible. Chop roughly.

❖ Trim the stalks from the chard leaves, slice into 2.5 cm/ 1 inch pieces and reserve.

❖ Heat the oil and butter in a heavy-based saucepan and gently fry the garlic and shallots for 1 minute. Add the chard stems, broad beans, parsley and savory and stir-fry for another minute. Stir in the cooked chard leaves and season to taste. Stir over a medium-low heat for 1-2 minutes, until well mixed. Allow to cool slightly then stir in the eggs and Parmesan.

❖ Divide the pastry into 8 then divide each piece in 2, one piece larger than the other.

❖ Roll each larger piece into a 18 cm/7 inch circle, cutting round a plate to neaten the edges. Use to line 8 x 10 cm/ 4 inch flan rings or pie tins, leaving the pastry to overlap the edge of the ring.

❖ Pile the filling into the pastry bases, then gather up the overlapping pastry to cover the filling partially. The pastry should come away from the edges of the ring to make a ball shape. Moisten the edges with water.

❖ Roll the smaller pieces of pastry into 9 cm/3½ inch circles and place on top of the bases. Brush with beaten egg yolk to glaze. Prick the surface with a fork.

❖ Bake at 180°C/375°F/gas mark 5 for 30 minutes until golden. Serve hot or at room temperature.

ROASTED ARTICHOKE, AUBERGINE, RED PEPPER AND GOAT CHEESE PIZZA

SERVES 4

THE CHILLI-FLAVOURED OIL AND ROASTED GARLIC GIVES THESE TOMATO-FREE PIZZAS ADDED ZEST.

6 oil-cured artichokes, quartered lengthways
2 small aubergines, sliced thinly
2 red peppers, deseeded and halved
4 large garlic cloves, unpeeled
½ tsp chilli powder

7 tbsp olive oil
Pizza Dough (page 110)
150 g/5 oz dry goat cheese, crumbled
100 g/4 oz mozzarella cheese, sliced
a few basil leaves, torn
salt and pepper

❖ Place the artichokes, aubergine slices, peppers and garlic cloves on an oiled baking sheet. Combine the chilli powder and olive oil and use a little to brush the aubergine slices. Reserve the rest.

❖ Bake in the oven at 200°C/400°F/ gas mark 6 for 20 minutes, turning the aubergines and brushing with oil.

❖ Remove the skins from the pepper and garlic. Slice the peppers into matchstick strips and mash the garlic.

❖ Divide the pizza dough into 4 balls. Roll each ball to flatten slightly. On a floured surface, slap and stretch each piece to form a 20 cm/8 inch circle. Place on floured baking sheets.

❖ Brush each circle with the remaining chilli and oil mixture. Smear with the garlic. Arrange the artichokes, aubergine slices and peppers on top. Add the cheeses and basil. Sprinkle with a little olive oil and season with salt and pepper. Bake at 240°C/ 475°F/gas mark 9 for about 15-20 minutes until the cheese is bubbling.

MUSHROOM, SAGE AND RICOTTA CANNELLONI WITH RED PEPPER SAUCE

SERVES 4

IT'S EASIER TO USE FLAT SHEETS OF LASAGNE RATHER THAN TUBES. ROLL THEM ROUND THE STUFFING AND BAKE SEAM-SIDE DOWN. IT TASTES BEST OF ALL MADE WITH HOME-MADE PASTA.

4 tbsp olive oil
100 g/ 4 oz flat mushrooms, chopped
400 g/14 oz ricotta cheese
2 tbsp pine kernels, toasted
2 tbsp sage, chopped finely

salt and pepper
8 lasagne sheets, cooked
Roasted Red Pepper Sauce (page 106)
2 tbsp freshly grated Parmesan

❖ Heat the oil in a pan and stir-fry the mushrooms for 5 minutes until the moisture has evaporated. Allow to cool.

❖ Mix the ricotta with the mushrooms, pine kernels and sage. Season to taste.

❖ Place some of the mixture down the centre of each lasagne sheet, rolling them into tubes. Reheat the sauce and pour a little into the base of a greased ovenproof dish. Add the tubes, seam-side down and pour over the remaining sauce. Sprinkle with the Parmesan, cover with foil and bake at 180°C/350°F/gas mark 4, for 20-30 minutes until heated through.

FARFALLE WITH BROAD BEANS AND GOAT CHEESE

SERVES 6

THE SUBTLE FLAVOUR OF SAVORY IS PERFECT WITH BROAD BEANS, BUT YOU COULD USE THYME INSTEAD. THE DISH IS FAIRLY RICH SO SERVE IT WITH A CRISP SALAD OF PUNGENT AND BITTER LEAVES, SUCH AS ESCAROLE, BATAVIA, ROCKET, WATERCRESS, SORREL AND CHICORY.

900 g/2 lb young broad beans, shelled
275 g/10 oz goat cheese
3 tbsp finely chopped savory
1 tbsp finely chopped parsley

3 tbsp extra virgin olive oil
350 g/12 oz farfalle
25 g/1 oz butter
1 garlic clove, chopped finely
salt and pepper

GARNISH
savory sprigs

❖ Blanch the beans for 2 minutes in a large saucepan of boiling water. Drain under cold running water. Peel away the tough outer skins.

❖ Beat the cheese with 2 tablespoons of the savory, the parsley, olive oil, salt and pepper.

❖ Boil the pasta in salted water until just cooked.

❖ Meanwhile, heat the butter in a small pan and gently fry the garlic and remaining savory for 1 minute. Add the broad beans and heat through. Season with salt and pepper.

❖ Drain the pasta and return to the pan. Stir in the cheese mixture. Transfer to a heated serving dish and scatter the beans on top. Garnish with savory sprigs.

GRILLED VEGETABLES IN FILO FLOWERS

SERVES 6

SERVE WARM AS A STARTER. MUSHROOMS AND AUBERGINES WOULD ALSO BE GOOD VEGETABLES TO USE.

4 sheets filo pastry, 45 x 30 cm/ 18 x 12 inches
olive oil for brushing
2 each small red and yellow peppers, cored, deseeded and halved

2 small courgettes, halved lengthways
3 baby artichokes bottled in oil, halved lengthways
salt and pepper

GARNISH
shavings of fresh Parmesan | *flat-leafed parsley*

❖ Lightly brush 6 x 150 ml/¼ pint ramekins with oil.

❖ Cut the filo into 24 x 15 cm/6 inch squares and cover with a damp cloth. Taking 4 squares at a time, brush each one with oil. Place 1 square on top of the next, twisting them so the corners are offset. Place in a ramekin, pressing well down. Repeat with the remaining squares.

❖ Bake at 190°C/375°F/gas mark 5 for 15-20 minutes until evenly browned. Carefully remove from the ramekins, place on a wire rack and keep warm.

❖ Meanwhile, brush the vegetables with oil and place skin side uppermost under a hot grill for 10-15 minutes until they begin to blacken.

❖ Remove the skins from the peppers then chop all the vegetables into bite-sized pieces.

❖ Fill each pastry case with pieces of vegetable. Season to taste and drizzle with a little olive oil.

❖ Garnish with Parmesan shavings and a parsley sprig.

CHARD AND CHEESE FILO PIE

SERVES 8

IF THE CHARD IS YOUNG, COOK THE STEMS WITH THE
LEAVES. OTHERWISE CUT AWAY THE STEMS AND DISCARD
THEM. YOU CAN USE SPINACH INSTEAD OF CHARD.

*900 g/2 lb Swiss chard or
spinach, lightly cooked and
drained
50 g/2 oz butter
2 leeks, halved lengthways and
thinly sliced
2 garlic cloves, finely chopped
2 tbsp finely chopped herbs
e.g. rosemary, thyme,
marjoram*

*2 tsp green peppercorns
grated zest of 1 orange
salt
225 g/8 oz goat cheese
225 g/8 oz ricotta or cottage
cheese
2 eggs, beaten
12 sheets filo pastry
olive oil for brushing
50 g/2 oz pine kernels, toasted*

❖ Squeeze as much liquid as possible from the chard, chop roughly and set aside.

❖ Melt the butter in a pan and gently fry the leeks for 2-3 minutes then add the garlic, herbs, peppercorns, orange zest and salt. Fry for 2-3 minutes.

❖ Remove to a bowl and combine with the chard, cheeses and eggs. Season with more salt if necessary.

❖ Place 1 sheet of filo in the bottom of a greased oven-proof dish measuring 23 x 30 cm/9 x 12 inches, trimming the filo to size if necessary. Brush with oil and sprinkle with a few pine kernels. Add 5 more sheets of filo, brushing each lightly with oil and scattering pine kernels between the layers.

❖ Pour the filling into the dish and level the surface. Cover with the remaining filo sheets, brushing them with oil and sprinkling with pine kernels. With a sharp knife cut through all the layers to make 7.5 cm/3 inch diamonds. Bake at 200°C/400°F/gas mark 6 for 40-50 minutes until browned and crisp.

FETTUCCINE WITH MUSHROOM AND HERB SAUCE

SERVES 4

FRESH MORELS, OR EVEN DRIED OR BOTTLED ONES,
MAKE THIS DISH OUT OF THIS WORLD. BUT IT'S STILL
PRETTY GOOD WITH A MIXTURE OF OTHER WILD OR
CULTIVATED MUSHROOMS.

*250 g/9 oz assorted mushrooms
(e.g. morels, chestnut, large flat
cap, shiitake, oyster), chopped
4 tbsp extra virgin olive oil
2 garlic cloves, chopped finely
2 tbsp finely chopped flat-leafed
parsley
1 tbsp finely chopped lovage*

*1 tbsp finely chopped chives
1 tbsp lemon juice
salt and pepper
350 g/12 oz fresh fettuccine
350 ml/12 fl oz whipping cream
50 g/2 oz pine kernels, toasted
3 tbsp basil leaves, torn*

❖ Stir-fry the mushrooms in the oil for 5 minutes until most of the liquid has evaporated. Add the garlic, parsley, lovage, chives, lemon juice, salt and pepper and stir-fry for another minute or two.

❖ Meanwhile, boil the fettuccine in a large pan of salted water for about 4 minutes, until tender but firm to bite. Drain and return to the pan.

❖ Stir in the cream, pine kernels, basil and several grindings of black pepper. Transfer to a heated serving dish and scatter the mushrooms on top.

TOMATO AND OLIVE BREAD

MAKES 2 LOAVES

TOMATO PASTE TURNS THE DOUGH INTO A PINK STICKY MESS. JUST KEEP KNEADING WITH FLOURED HANDS AND IT WILL EVENTUALLY BECOME SPRINGY AGAIN. SPRAYING WITH WATER DURING BAKING GIVES THE LOAF A LOVELY CRISP CRUST.

700g/1½ lb strong white flour	*400 ml/14 fl oz tepid water*
1½ tsp salt	*6 tbsp tomato paste*
½ tbsp sugar	*20 oil-cured black olives, pitted*
1 sachet easy-blend dried yeast	*and halved*
1 tbsp olive oil	*50 g/2 oz pumpkin seeds*
	flour for dusting

❖ Sift the flour, salt, sugar and yeast in a large bowl. Make a well in the centre and gradually stir in the oil and water to form a soft dough. Knead for at least 15 minutes until smooth and springy.

❖ Transfer to a large oiled bowl and cover with cling film. Leave to rise in a warm place for 1-2 hours until doubled in size.

❖ Flatten the risen dough, spread the tomato paste, olives and pumpkin seeds over it. Dust with flour, roll up and knead again until smooth.

❖ Divide the dough in half and place in 2 greased and floured loaf tins. Dust with flour, cover and leave to rise for 45-60 minutes until doubled in size.

❖ Bake at 200°C/400°F/gas mark 6 for 40-45 minutes, spraying with water 3 times during the first 10 minutes of cooking.

RICOTTA AND BASIL TART WITH SUN-DRIED TOMATOES AND OLIVES

SERVES 6

A LIGHT-TEXTURED TART WITH A RICH SHORTCRUST PASTRY CASE. THE PARMESAN CHEESE AND OLIVES ARE QUITE SALTY SO YOU WILL NOT NEED TO ADD ANY EXTRA TO THE FILLING.

PASTRY

175 g/6 oz plain flour	*1 egg yolk*
½ tsp salt	*1 tbsp cold water*
100 g//4 oz butter	

FILLING

50 g/2 oz torn basil leaves	*5 tbsp whipping cream*
2 tbsp olive oil	*25 g/1 oz oil-cured sun-dried*
350 g/12 oz ricotta	*tomatoes, chopped*
3 tbsp grated Parmesan cheese	*10 oil-cured black olives, pitted*
3 eggs	*and chopped*

❖ Sift the flour and salt into a bowl and rub in the butter. Mix in the egg yolk and water to form a smooth dough. Cover with cling-film and chill for 30 minutes.

❖ Roll out thinly and use to line a 24-25 cm/9½-10 inch flan ring. Line the ring with foil and baking beans and bake blind at 200°C/400°F/gas mark 6 for 8 minutes. Remove the foil and beans and bake for another 5-7 minutes until the edges are just golden. Allow to cool.

❖ Put the basil, oil and cheeses in a food processor. Season with pepper and process until just mixed. Add the eggs and cream and process again. Stir in the sun-dried tomatoes and olives but do not process.

❖ Pour the mixture into the pie shell and bake at 200°C/400°F/gas mark 6 for 40-45 minutes until set. Serve hot or at room temperature.

CHICK-PEA CREPES

MAKES 8

CHICK-PEA, OR GRAM FLOUR AS IT IS OFTEN CALLED, MAKES BEAUTIFUL LACY CREPE-LIKE PANCAKES BUT THEY NEED CAREFUL HANDLING. USE A LITTLE MORE OIL THAN USUAL AND MAKE SURE IT IS REALLY HOT. THE PANCAKES ARE QUITE PUNGENT BECAUSE OF THE CHILLI, SO A COOLING YOGURT-BASED SAUCE IS A WELCOME ACCOMPANIMENT.

225 g/8 oz chick-pea flour	*2 fresh green chillies, deseeded*
2 tsp salt	*and chopped finely*
2 tsp black sesame seeds	*600 ml/1 pint cold water*
1 tsp turmeric	*groundnut oil for frying*
¼ tsp ground black pepper	

TO SERVE

A yogurt-based sauce e.g.:	*Cucumber and Mango Raita*
Coriander Sauce (page 107)	*(page 109)*
Minted Yogurt Sauce (page 107)	

❖ Sift the flour and salt into a bowl and combine with the spices and chilli. Make a well in the centre and gradually whisk in the water, drawing in the flour from the edge, until you have a smooth batter. Cover and leave to stand for 30 minutes. Whisk again just before using.

❖ Heat 2-3 teaspoons of oil in a heavy-based non-stick 20-23 cm/8-9 inch frying pan until just smoking.

❖ Pour in a ladleful of batter with a circular motion so that the batter is distributed right to the edges. Immediately smooth the top with a spatula, spreading the batter evenly. Lift the edge when it has just set and let any surplus batter run underneath. Fry over a fairly high heat for about 50 seconds each side. Interleave each cooked pancake with a paper towel, cover with a plate and keep warm while you cook the rest.

❖ Carefully fold the pancakes into 4 and serve with a yogurt-based sauce.

THREE-CHEESE CALZONI

SERVES 4

CALZONI ARE ITALIAN TURNOVERS MADE WITH VERY THIN PIZZA DOUGH. THEY CAN BE BAKED IN THE OVEN BUT FRYING MAKES THEM PUFFY AND CRISP. SERVE AS A STARTER OR WITH A TOMATO SAUCE AS A MAIN COURSE.

Pizza Dough (page 110)

FILLING

225 g/8 oz ricotta cheese, sieved	*1 egg, lightly beaten*
150 g/5 oz mozzarella cheese,	*2 large tomatoes, skinned,*
diced	*deseeded and chopped*
50 g/2 oz freshly grated	*¼ tsp black pepper*
Parmesan	*3 tbsp chopped basil*

❖ Combine the filling ingredients and set aside.

❖ Place the risen dough on a floured surface and knead for a few minutes. Divide into 12 pieces and roll each into a ball. Roll out to a 3 mm/⅛ inch thick circle, neatening the edges by cutting round an upturned bowl.

❖ Place a scant 2 tablespoons of filling on half of the circle, leaving a narrow border. Moisten the edge, fold over and seal. Leave in a warm place for 15 minutes.

❖ Heat 2.5 cm/1 inch of oil in a large frying pan until very hot. Fry a few calzoni at a time for 2-3 minutes each side until golden brown. Keep warm in a hot oven while you fry the rest. Serve immediately.

COURGETTE AND CORIANDER GOUGERE

SERVES 4

A SPECTACULARLY COLOURFUL DISH WHICH IS SIMPLE TO PREPARE. USE SMALL GREEN COURGETTES ABOUT 12.5 CM/5 INCHES LONG.

CHOUX PASTRY

75 g/3 oz butter	*100 g/4 oz plain flour*
200 ml/7 fl oz water	*2 eggs*
¼ tsp salt	*1 egg white*
cayenne	*50 g/2 oz Red Leicester cheese,*
½ tsp cumin seeds, toasted	*grated*

FILLING

25 g/1 oz butter	*2 tsp lemon juice*
2 shallots, chopped finely	*1 tbsp finely chopped coriander*
2 garlic cloves, chopped finely	*salt and pepper*
20 g/¾ oz plain flour	*6 small courgettes, trimmed and*
¼ tsp turmeric	*sliced lengthways into thin*
300 ml/½ pint milk	*strips*

❖ Put the butter, water, salt, cayenne and cumin in a saucepan and stir until the butter has melted. Bring just to the boil and remove from the heat. Add the flour all at once and beat vigorously with a wooden spoon until the mixture pulls away from the sides of the pan. Beat for 1 minute over a very low heat, then allow to cool slightly.

❖ Lightly beat the eggs and egg white together. Gradually beat into the mixture with the cheese until very smooth and glossy.

❖ Using a plain 1 cm/½ inch nozzle, pipe 2 circles of mixture, one on top of the other, round the edge of four 14 cm/5½ inch diameter greased ovenproof dishes. Bake at 220°C/425°F/gas mark 7 for about 25 minutes until golden and puffed.

❖ Meanwhile, melt the butter in a saucepan and gently fry the shallots and garlic for 3-4 minutes. Add the flour and turmeric. Cook, stirring, for 1 minute. Add the milk, bring to the boil, stirring constantly until thickened. Simmer for 5 minutes over a very low heat, stirring. Add the lemon juice and coriander and season to taste.

❖ Steam the courgette slices over boiling water for 5 minutes until just tender. Arrange them in the choux rings. Pour over the sauce and serve immediately.

BLACK BEAN TACOS WITH ROAST CORN CHILLI SAUCE

SERVES 4 - 8

TACOS ARE CRISP-FRIED TORTILLAS. YOU CAN BUY THEM READY-MADE BUT IT'S BETTER TO FRY THE TORTILLAS YOURSELF. TORTILLAS ARE TRADITIONALLY MADE WITH MASA HARINA – DEHYDRATED MAIZE FLOUR. IT'S DEFINITELY EASIER TO USE STORE-BOUGHT TORTILLAS.

2 tbsp olive oil
1 onion, chopped finely
4 garlic cloves, chopped finely
4 fresh chillies, deseeded and chopped
2 tsp ground cumin
1 tbsp dried oregano
450 g/1 lb cooked black beans (225 g/8 oz dry weight)

100 g/ 4 oz frozen sweetcorn kernels
400 g/14 oz can chopped tomatoes
300 ml/½ pint Vegetable Stock (page 111)
salt and pepper
groundnut oil, for frying
8 tortillas

TO SERVE
Roasted Corn Chilli Sauce (page 107)

❖ Heat the oil in a pan and gently fry the onion and garlic for 5 minutes until translucent. Add the chilli, cumin and oregano and stir-fry for a minute to release the flavour.

❖ Stir in the remaining ingredients, bring to the boil and simmer for 20 minutes, stirring occasionally, until most of the liquid has evaporated.

❖ Shallow-fry the tortillas in very hot oil for 30 seconds until slightly browned. Drain on paper towels and keep warm while you fry the rest.

❖ Form each tortilla into a boat shape in the palm of your hand, spoon in some of the filling and top with the heated sauce. They will become crisp as you do so.

❖ Transfer to a warm serving dish into which all the tacos will just fit and serve immediately.

CHILLI AND CORIANDER CORN MUFFINS

MAKES 8

ROASTED GARLIC AND CHILLI GIVE THESE QUICKLY MADE MUFFINS A SPICY KICK. FOR THE BEST RESULTS, BAKE THEM IN INDIVIDUAL HIGH-SIDED PIE TINS. OTHERWISE USE YORKSHIRE PUDDING TINS.

2 large fresh green chillies
3 large garlic cloves, unpeeled
225 g/8 oz plain flour
100 g/4 oz yellow cornmeal or polenta
1 tbsp baking powder
3 eggs

5 tbsp olive oil
5 tbsp finely chopped coriander
2 tsp muscovado sugar
1 tsp salt
175 ml/6 fl oz water

❖ Roast the chillies and garlic at 180°C/350°F/gas mark 5 for 15 minutes. Discard the skins and the chilli seeds and chop roughly. Place 8 oiled individual pie tins in the oven for 5 minutes.

❖ Sift the flour, cornmeal and baking powder in a bowl.

❖ Put the chilli and garlic in a blender with the eggs, oil, coriander, sugar and salt. Add the water and process briefly until smooth. Add to the dry ingredients, whisking well to form a smooth batter.

❖ Divide the batter amongst the hot pie tins and bake for 15-20 minutes.

SALSA VERDE (PIQUANT GREEN SAUCE)

MAKES ABOUT 250 ML/9 FL OZ

3 shallots, chopped
9 tbsp finely chopped parsley
6 tbsp finely chopped basil
3 tbsp capers, rinsed
2 garlic cloves, crushed

grated zest of 1½ lemons
1½ tbsp lemon juice
175 ml/6 fl oz olive oil
salt and pepper

❖ Combine all the ingredients in a blender and process until smooth. Check the seasoning and add more salt and pepper if necessary. The sauce will keep in an airtight container in the refrigerator for 1 week. Allow to come to room temperature before serving.

ROASTED RED PEPPER SAUCE

MAKES 600ML/1 PINT

4 red peppers
2 tbsp olive oil
1 onion, chopped finely
2 tsp finely chopped thyme
2 garlic cloves, chopped finely
4 tomatoes, peeled, deseeded
and chopped

1 tbsp white wine vinegar
300 ml/½ pint Vegetable Stock
(page 111)
salt and pepper
20 g/¾ oz butter

❖ Place the peppers under a hot grill for about 15 minutes, turning frequently, until the skins begin to blister on all sides. Allow to cool then remove the skins and seeds and chop the flesh.
❖ Heat the oil in a saucepan and gently fry the onion and thyme for 5 minutes until the onion is translucent. Add the garlic and fry for another minute or two. Stir in the tomatoes, vinegar, stock, salt and pepper.
❖ Purée the mixture with the peppers by rubbing through a sieve. Return to the pan, bring to the boil and reduce slightly, then whisk in the butter.
❖ Check the seasoning and serve either hot or at room temperature.

TANGY PEANUT SAUCE

MAKES 200ML/7 FL OZ

75 g/3 oz peanuts, chopped
finely
1 tbsp wine vinegar

1 tbsp tamari (Japanese soy
sauce)
225 ml/8 fl oz water

❖ Put all the ingredients in a food processor and blend until smooth.
❖ Pour into a saucepan and simmer over a medium-low heat, stirring, for 15 minutes until thickened.

CORIANDER SAUCE

MAKES 300ML/ ½ PINT

75 g/3 oz fresh coriander,
trimmed
25 g/1 oz flat-leafed parsley,
trimmed
2 spring onions, chopped
1 garlic clove, crushed

2 tbsp lime juice
1½ tsp toasted cumin seeds
¼ tsp salt
pepper to taste
75 ml/3 fl oz Greek yogurt
75 ml/3 fl oz double cream

❖ Combine all the ingredients, except the yogurt and cream, in a food processor and purée for 3 minutes, scraping the sides of the bowl frequently. Pour into a bowl and stir in the yogurt and cream.

MINTED YOGURT SAUCE

MAKES 300ML/ ½ PINT

300 ml/½ pint Greek yogurt
1 garlic clove, crushed
1 tsp olive oil

½ tsp wine vinegar
salt and pepper
4 tbsp finely chopped mint

❖ Combine the ingredients in the order listed. Cover and leave to stand for 1 hour before serving.

ROAST CORN CHILLI SAUCE

MAKES 425ML/ ¾ PINT

2 ears sweetcorn with husks
2 fresh green chillies
2 tbsp vegetable oil
½ onion, chopped
1 garlic clove, chopped finely
250 ml/9 fl oz Vegetable Stock
(page 111)

300 ml/½ pint single cream
25 g/1 oz coriander, stalks
removed
2 tbsp lime juice
salt

❖ Heat the oven to 180°C/350°F/gas mark 4 and roast the corn in their husks for 10 minutes, turning occasionally. Add the chillies and roast for another 10 minutes.
❖ Allow to cool then remove the husks and cut the kernels from the cobs. Cut each cob stalk into 3 pieces. Peel the chillies and remove the seeds.
❖ Heat the oil in a saucepan and gently fry the cob stalks, onion and garlic for 3-4 minutes until the onion is translucent. Add the stock, raise the heat and simmer for 10 minutes until the liquid is reduced slightly.
❖ Add the cream and simmer for 10 minutes, stirring continuously as the liquid reduces.
❖ Remove the cob pieces with a slotted spoon, scraping off as much sauce as possible. Add to the sauce two-thirds of the corn kernels, the chillies, coriander and lime juice. Liquidise in a blender until smooth. Stir in the remaining kernels. Season with salt to taste, reheat and serve.

TOMATO SAUCE

MAKES 375ML/13 FL OZ

400 g/14 oz can chopped tomatoes
60 g/2½ oz butter
1 onion, halved
1 small strip lemon peel

1 garlic clove, chopped finely
2 tsp dried oregano
¼ tsp sugar
salt and pepper

❖ Put all the ingredients in a saucepan. Simmer over a low heat for 45 minutes, uncovered, stirring occasionally. Discard the onion and lemon peel and pour the mixture into a food processor. Blend until smooth then return to the pan. Check the seasoning, adding more salt, pepper or sugar as necessary.

SATAY SAUCE

MAKES 425ML/¾ PINT

100 g/4 oz fresh peanuts, roasted
2 tsp coriander seeds, roasted
2 tsp vegetable oil
2 garlic cloves, chopped finely
1 shallot or ½ small onion, chopped finely
2 tsp finely chopped lemon grass (or ½ tsp dried)

½ tsp chilli powder
1 tsp ground cumin seeds
450 ml/¾ pint water
1 tsp Indonesian soy sauce
1 tsp dark brown sugar
½ tsp salt
juice of ½ lime or lemon
2 tbsp yogurt
freshly ground black pepper

❖ Put the peanuts and coriander seeds in a coffee grinder or blender and grind as finely as possible.
❖ Heat the oil in a saucepan. Add the garlic, shallot, lemon grass, chilli powder and cumin. Stir-fry for about 1 minute until lightly browned.
❖ Add the water, soy sauce, sugar, salt and peanut mixture. Bring to the boil, stirring. Reduce the heat and simmer for 15-20 minutes until thickened, stirring frequently.
❖ Allow to cool slightly then stir lemon in the lime juice, yogurt and black pepper.

SPICY GINGER AND SESAME SAUCE

MAKES 150ML/¼ PINT

2 tsp sesame seeds
50 g/2 oz peeled fresh ginger root, chopped finely
4 tbsp rice vinegar (or wine vinegar)

2½ tbsp sugar
1 tbsp tamari (Japanese soy sauce)
¼ tsp salt
1 tsp snipped chives

❖ Dry-fry the sesame seeds in a small heavy-based pan until they turn golden. Remove from the pan and set aside.
❖ Put the ginger, vinegar, sugar, tamari and salt in a small bowl and blend together until smooth and the sugar has dissolved.
❖ Pour into a small serving bowl and stir in the sesame seeds and chives.
❖ Leave to stand at room temperature for at least 1 hour.

PEANUT SAUCE

MAKES 350ML/12 FL OZ

1 tbsp groundnut oil
1 onion, chopped finely
½ green pepper, chopped finely
1 garlic clove, chopped finely
100 g/4 oz tomatoes, peeled and chopped
50 g/2 oz finely chopped peanuts
½ tsp salt
pepper
150 ml/¼ pint milk
2 tsp tamari (Japanese soy sauce)

❖ Heat the oil in a saucepan and gently fry the onion and green pepper for 10 minutes. Add the garlic and tomatoes and simmer for 10 minutes more, stirring occasionally.
❖ Liquidise in a blender with the nuts, salt and pepper.
❖ Return to the pan, add the milk and simmer, uncovered for 10 minutes, stirring occasionally.
❖ Stir in the tamari just before serving.

CARROT AND CORIANDER RELISH

MAKES 150ML/¼ PINT

90 g/3 ½ oz grated carrot
15 g/½ oz trimmed coriander
25 g/1 oz onion, chopped
2.5 cm/1 inch piece fresh root ginger, chopped finely
1 green chilli, deseeded and chopped finely
2 tbsp lemon juice
1 tbsp sugar
½ tsp salt

❖ Combine all the ingredients in a food processor and blend until smooth. Leave to stand at room temperature for at least 1 hour to let the flavours develop.

OLIVE AND CORIANDER RELISH

SERVES 4

2 red peppers
175 g/6 oz black olives in oil, stoned and sliced finely
½ fresh green chilli, deseeded and chopped very finely
6 tbsp finely chopped coriander leaves
1 tbsp lemon juice
pepper
5 tbsp olive oil
lettuce leaves
1 hard-boiled egg, quartered

❖ Place the peppers under a hot grill for 10 minutes, turning occasionally, until the skins begin to blacken. Cover or place in a sealed plastic bag for 5 minutes. Remove the skin and seeds and cut the flesh into small dice. Mix with the olives, chilli and coriander in a bowl.
❖ Whisk together the lemon juice, pepper and olive oil and pour over the olive mixture. Allow to stand at room temperature for 1 hour.
❖ Pile the mixture on a bed of lettuce leaves and top with the hard-boiled egg quarters.

CUCUMBER AND MANGO RAITA

MAKES 350ML/12 FL OZ

75 g/3 oz peeled and finely chopped cucumber
½ tsp salt
1 large ripe mango
150 ml/¼ pint set yogurt

2 spring onions, green part included, chopped finely
2 tbsp lime juice
pepper

❖ Sprinkle the cucumber with the salt and drain for 30 minutes.
❖ Chop the mango flesh and mix with the drained cucumber and remaining ingredients.
❖ Leave to stand for 1 hour before serving.

PEAR AND WALNUT OIL DRESSING

MAKES ABOUT 100 ML/3 ½ FL OZ

100 g/4 oz peeled and cored ripe pears, chopped roughly
1 tbsp lemon juice
2 tbsp walnut oil

2 tbsp olive oil
1½ tsp green peppercorns
salt

❖ Put all the ingredients in a blender and process until smooth.

HAZELNUT AND ORANGE VINAIGRETTE

MAKES 100ML/3 ½ FL OZ

2 tbsp orange juice
1 tsp white wine vinegar
salt and pepper

2 cm/¾ inch piece fresh ginger root
4 tbsp hazelnut oil

❖ Combine the orange juice, vinegar, salt and pepper in a small bowl. Put the peeled ginger in a garlic press and squeeze the juice into the dressing. Whisk in the oil.

PIZZA DOUGH

MAKES 2 X 30 CM/12 INCH OR 4 X 20 CM/8 INCH BASES

375 g/13 oz strong white flour
1½ tsp salt
1 sachet easy-blend dried yeast

1 tbsp extra virgin olive oil
225 ml/8 fl oz tepid water

❖ Sift the flour, salt and yeast into a bowl. Make a well in the centre and pour in the oil and water. Stir vigorously, gradually drawing in the flour, to form a soft dough.
❖ Knead on a floured surface for at least 10 minutes until the dough feels silky smooth and springy.
❖ Place in an oiled bowl, turning the dough so it is covered with oil, and cover with cling film. Leave to rise in a warm place for up to 2 hours until doubled in size.

VEGETABLE STOCK

MAKES ABOUT 1.75 LITRES/3 PINTS

2 tbsp sunflower oil
3 onions, chopped
15 g/½ oz each fresh parsley, tarragon, basil and thyme, chopped finely
2 courgettes, sliced finely
1 fennel bulb, chopped finely
2 leeks, green parts included, sliced finely

2 celery sticks, leaves included, sliced finely
4 garlic cloves, peeled and left whole
10 black peppercorns, coarsely crushed
1 tsp salt

❖ Heat the oil in a large saucepan. Add the onions and herbs and gently fry for 5 minutes until the onion is translucent.
❖ Add the remaining ingredients, then cover and sweat together over a low heat for 10-15 minutes, stirring occasionally.
❖ Add 2 litres/3½ pints of water, bring to the boil, skim and simmer, half-covered, for 30 minutes.
❖ Strain through a muslin-lined sieve. The stock can be refrigerated for up to 5 days.

STRONG VEGETABLE STOCK

MAKES ABOUT 2 LITRES/3 ½ PINTS

2 tbsp sunflower oil
2 onions, chopped finely
2 leeks, green parts included, sliced finely
3 carrots, sliced finely
3 celery sticks, sliced finely
1 celeriac, chopped
4 tomatoes, chopped
1 potato, chopped
½ small cabbage, chopped finely

100 g/4 oz mushrooms, chopped finely
6 garlic cloves, peeled
2 bay leaves
50 g/2 oz parsley, chopped roughly
3 sprigs thyme or marjoram
1 tsp salt
10 black peppercorns, coarsely crushed

❖ Heat the oil in a large pan. Add all the ingredients and 300 ml/½ pint water. Cover and simmer over a medium-low heat for 15 minutes. Add 2.3 litres/4 pints water, bring to the boil, then simmer, half covered, for 1½ hours, stirring from time to time.
❖ Strain through a muslin-lined sieve. Check the flavour, adding more seasoning if necessary. Reduce the stock further if you want a stronger flavour. It can be refrigerated for up to 5 days.

Index